Margaret [illegible]

1988

# *Dickens and the Suspended Quotation*

# *Dickens and the Suspended Quotation*

MARK LAMBERT

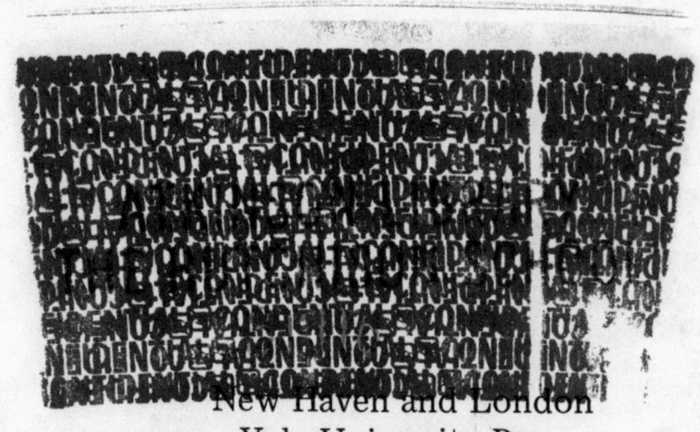

New Haven and London
Yale University Press

Published with assistance from the Kingsley Trust Association Publication Fund established by the Scroll and Key Society of Yale College.



Designed by Nancy Ovedovitz and set in IBM Century type. Printed in the United States of America by Halliday Lithograph Corp., West Hanover, Mass.

**Library of Congress Cataloging in Publication Data**

Lambert, Mark, 1942–
Dickens and the suspended quotation.

Includes bibliographical references and index.
1. Dickens, Charles, 1812–1870—Style.
2. Direct discourse in literature. I. Title.
PR4594.L35 823′.8 80-22072
ISBN 0-300-02555-6

10 9 8 7 6 5 4 3 2 1

For Ellen

# *Contents*

# *Acknowledgments*

My greatest debt is to my wife. "For Ellen" seems almost presumptuous: but for her there would be no book to dedicate.

Through the time I spent on this project and, indeed, for the past eighteen years, Professor Marie Borroff has been teaching me about style: to make distinctions that are nice in the modern sense, to ignore distinctions nice only in Chaucer's sense.

At just the right moment—early but not too early in my work on Dickens's quotations—I lectured on the topic at Cornell University. I remember that evening with pleasure and wish to thank Professors Reeve Parker and Edgar Rosenberg, their colleagues and students for a delightful and very useful discussion.

For detailed (and sometimes radical) criticism of one version or another of this essay, I am grateful to Professors Irma Brandeis of Bard College, Roger Brown of Harvard University, George H. Ford of the University of Rochester, Thomas M. Greene and Martin Price of Yale University.

The last steps on the path from strange idea to bound volume were made pleasant and sure by Ellen Graham and Lawrence Kenney, my editors at the Yale University Press. Earlier steps were made easy—and, indeed, possible—by my colleagues at Bard College, who generously arranged and arranged and rearranged so that I might take several leaves.

I end this list, as I began it, with a debt in the family. Several long distance calls to my brother David Lambert allowed me to disguise my ignorance of statistical method—or at least I hope they did.

# *Texts Cited and Abbreviations*

## 1. DICKENS

The volumes of the Oxford Illustrated Dickens are probably available to more readers than those of any other collected edition, and I cite the OID texts except in those rare cases (always indicated) where I have preferred a different reading. Page references are to the OID volumes, and the abbreviations I use for volumes in this edition are:

| | |
|---|---|
| *AN* | *American Notes and Pictures from Italy* |
| *BH* | *Bleak House* |
| *BR* | *Barnaby Rudge* |
| *CB* | *Christmas Books* |
| *CS* | *Christmas Stories* |
| *DC* | *David Copperfield* |
| *DS* | *Dombey and Son* |
| *ED* | *The Mystery of Edwin Drood* |
| *GE* | *Great Expectations* |
| *HT* | *Hard Times* |
| *LD* | *Little Dorrit* |
| *MC* | *Martin Chuzzlewit* |
| *MHC* | *Master Humphrey's Clock and A Child's History of England* |
| *NN* | *Nicholas Nickleby* |
| *OCS* | *The Old Curiosity Shop* |
| *OMF* | *Our Mutual Friend* |
| *OT* | *Oliver Twist* |
| *PP* | *Pickwick Papers* |
| *SB* | *Sketches by Boz* |
| *TTC* | *A Tale of Two Cities* |
| *UT* | *The Uncommercial Traveller and Reprinted Pieces* |

I have used the following editions of works not included in the Oxford Illustrated Dickens:

*The Plays and Poems of Charles Dickens.* Edited by Richard Herne Shepherd. 2 vols. London, 1885.
*Charles Dickens: the Public Readings.* Edited by Philip Collins. Oxford, 1975.
*Charles Dickens' Uncollected Writings from Household Words, 1850–1859.* Edited with an Introduction and Notes by Harry Stone. 2 vols. Bloomington, 1968.
*The Letters of Charles Dickens.* Pilgrim Edition. Edited by Madeline House and Graham Storey. Oxford, 1965–.

The two major biographies of Dickens, cited throughout by the authors' surnames, are:

John Forster. *The Life of Charles Dickens.* New Edition, with Notes and an Index by A. J. Hoppe and Additional Footnotes. 2 vols. New York, 1966.
Edgar Johnson. *Charles Dickens: His Tragedy and Triumph.* 2 vols. New York, 1952.

## 2. OTHER NINETEENTH-CENTURY NOVELISTS

I have used the following editions except where otherwise noted.

William Harrison Ainsworth. *Windsor Castle.* London, n.d.
Jane Austen. *Emma.* Edited by Stephen M. Parrish. New York, 1972.
Charlotte Brontë. *Jane Eyre.* Edited by Richard J. Dunn. New York, 1971.
Emily Brontë. *Wuthering Heights.* With a Critical Supplement and an Afterword by Baruch Hochman. New York, 1974.
Edward George Bulwer-Lytton. *Pelham: or the Adventures of a Gentleman.* Edited with an Introduction by Jerome J. McGann. Lincoln, Nebraska, 1972.
Lewis Carroll. *Alice's Adventures in Wonderland and Through the Looking-Glass.* With a Foreword by Horace Gregory. New York, 1960.
Wilkie Collins. *The Woman in White.* Edited with an Introduction and Notes by Julian Symonds. Baltimore, 1974; reprinted 1977.
Benjamin Disraeli. *Sybil: or the Two Nations.* With an Introduction by Walter Sichel. London, 1926; reprinted 1970.

——. *Vivian Grey*. With an Introduction by Philip Guedalla. New York, 1926.

Maria Edgeworth. *Castle Rackrent.* New York, 1965.

George Eliot. *Adam Bede.* With an Introduction by Gordon S. Haight. New York, 1948; reprinted 1964.

John Galt. *Annals of the Parish.* Edited with an Introduction by James Kinsley. London, 1972.

Elizabeth Gaskell. *Mary Barton: A Tale of Manchester Life.* Edited with an Introduction by Stephen Gill. Baltimore, 1970.

Henry James. *The Portrait of a Lady*. With an Introduction by Fred B. Millett. New York, 1951.

Charles Kingsley. *Yeast*. In *The Works of Charles Kingsley*, vol. 4. London, 1899.

Frederick Marryat. "How to Write a Fashionable Novel." In *Nineteenth Century British Novelists on the Novel*, edited by George L. Barnett, pp. 62–76. New York, 1971.

Thomas Love Peacock. *Nightmare Abbey and Crotchet Castle.* With an Introduction by J. B. Priestley. London, 1947.

Sir Walter Scott. *The Heart of Midlothian.* With an Introduction by David Daiches. New York, 1948; reprinted 1967.

——. *Waverley*. In *The Waverley Novels of Sir Walter Scott, Bart.* Edinburgh, 1859–60.

Mary Shelley. *Frankenstein.* New York, 1965.

Robert Smith Surtees. *Handley Cross.* London, 1892.

——. *Jorrocks' Jaunts and Jollities.* With an Essay on Surtees by Bonamy Dobree. London, 1928; reprinted 1971.

William Makepeace Thackeray. *The Complete Works.* With Introductions by William P. Trent and John Bell. New York, 1905.

Anthony Trollope. *An Autobiography.* With an Introduction by Michael Sadleir. London, 1953; reprinted 1968.

——. *Can You Forgive Her?* With an Introduction by Simon Raven. New York, 1977.

——. *Doctor Thorne.* New York, 1962.

——. *The Duke's Children.* With an Introduction by Simon Raven. New York, 1977.

——. *The Eustace Diamonds.* 2 vols. New York, 1942.

——. *Framley Parsonage.* London, 1906; reprinted 1932.

Mark Twain. *Adventures of Huckleberry Finn.* With an Introduction and Notes by Henry Nash Smith. Boston, 1958.

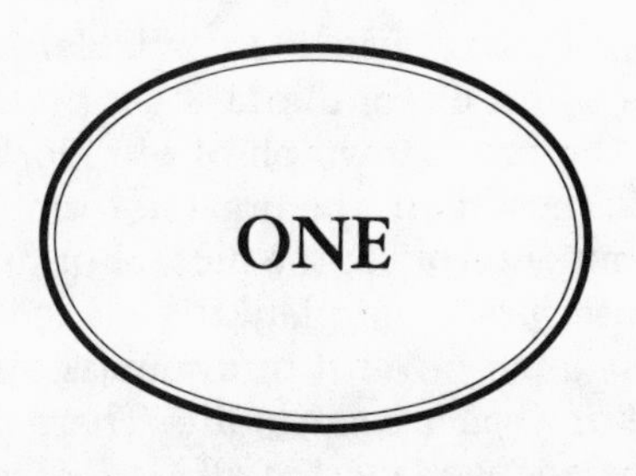

# ONE

# *Quoting Directly: Choices*

"Never mind," returned the Captain, though he was evidently dismayed by the figures; "all's fish that comes to your net, I suppose?"

"Certainly," said Mr. Brogley. "But sprats an't whales, you know."

The philosophy of this observation seemed to strike the Captain.

*Dombey and Son*

Whales there are in Dickens, and a multitude of sprats. This is a book about plankton. An explanation is called for, and called for the more loudly because my main business is neither with the reader who simply and fervently wishes to learn all that can be known about this one novelist, nor with the reader primarily interested in historical linguistics. Rather I address those who care about Dickens, but not necessarily more than they care about Dante, Shakespeare, or Tolstoy; who will look closely at the way great writers use language and have a general interest in questions about language but see no reason (as indeed there is none) to allow stylistics a special claim to interpretive power. [1] In these first pages, and then in this study as a whole, I must suggest why, when life is short and there are many writers we might be learning from and about, and when in any great writer there are dozens of whales and hundreds of sprats one might be studying, it can be a delight to think about, construct models for, and count, and circle around, Charles Dickens's use of a particular kind of sentence in a fair number of his direct quotations: the sort of sentence exemplified by the first paragraph of our *Dombey* epigraph.

I can give you, first of all, the organic form or ecological suasion to such an enterprise; the metaphor here is an appealing one, and those sprats and plankton make it irresistible. Dickens, like any great novelist or dramatist or epic poet, is a sea, and the life of a sea is a single life. There is the food chain and the interdependency of all God's creatures: if plankton demography has changed, watch for shifts in the sprat population; if sprats are no longer what they were, look to the whales. This is a metaphor rather than an argument and as long as it remains a metaphor it is safe both from refutation and from precise employment. I will leave it here in the company of the Song of Sixpence rather than Hegel; that is, I will not claim that the present work contributes anything toward a proof of the rightness of the organic form idea. What I think I can do, for some of you, is show how powerful that old metaphor remains, what pleasures there are in the proceeding on (rather than coming to a conclusion from) the hypothesis that a stylistic feature *means,* is message rather than noise.

But the other thing I must stress here is that those who spend time studying plankton do so not primarily because they are convinced (either by argument or metaphor) that through plankton one comes to whales, but because they find plankton fascinating as plankton. With stylistics, as with any decision to spend time in *this* rather than *that* area of humane studies, there is a real, though not always clear, demarcation between *us* and *them,* and it must be acknowledged that *we* have neither a more profound vision of truth nor a greater sense of duty than *they* have: we merely have different pleasures. It follows, reader, that if you are one of *them,* you may certainly be excused from reading the present study; this book would teach you some things about Dickens you don't know at present, but there are other books and articles which would teach you other things you don't know and would be happier to learn. On the other hand, I do think reading the book at hand is a good way to find out if you *are* one of us.

And who are we, the plankton specialists? Well, I confess that this metaphor is in my case really metonymy. Indeed I suspect most of *us* were fascinated by our first look at real plankton or real paramecia. Basically, stylistics has much the same kind of attraction as microscopy, grows from the same sense of wonder. One takes two drops of water—identical, it seems, empty, pure—and fixes them over the wells of a slide; focuses; studies first one, then the other. You remember what the experience is like. Form after form appears, there are different sorts of motion, different populations of beasties in the two drops. And of course the longer one looks, the more one sees; the more one looks (to reverse our figure) the more one is able to *read* in each of the droplets. No, the point is not at all that the paramecium is a more interesting creature than the sprat or the whale; the primitive fascination of stylistics, of literary microscopy, is the fascination of seeing more and more things swarming and changing *where there had seemed to be nothing at all*. That discovery of something in nothing, that first dialing of Eden 001, qualified the whole experience of stylistic investigation and makes it different from the seeing more and more which is common to all forms of literary study. Learning things here is quite different from, let us say, being taught things about Dante by Charles Singleton. Professor Singleton is almost indispensable; every reader must see more in Dante's portrayal of Satan after looking at Singleton's commentary than he saw before. But only the most naive reader will have reached the end of the *Inferno* without realizing there must be a great deal to learn about this Dantesque Satan; we know Dante is like that, know that his description will have meaning of that kind, even if we don't know what that meaning is or how much of it there is.[2] On the other hand, one might be a quite excellent Dickensian and be surprised by the factual sections of the present study; one most likely has simply not thought about whether Dickens is or is not like that because in the present case the *that* is a new sort of thing to observe. To say this, unfortunately, is not really to boast. One imagines, for instance, that Dante would have approved of most or all of what Professor Singleton wrote about the *Inferno*'s Satan. Dickens, whom I love and revere, would most certainly not have liked the present book. He would have said those drops of water were empty, I suspect, and that staring at drops of water was an unwholesome activity. But he would have been wrong—wrong, at least, about the emptiness of the drops.

In any case, our particular concern here is with the strong taste of certain early Victorian novelists—and the particularly strong taste of the younger Dickens—for a certain form of direct quotation: the form Dickens employs when giving us Captain Cuttle's words in our *Dombey* epigraph. Before long I'll provide something better than this ostensive definition of our main object of study; but not just yet. I want to glance first at some methodological problems raised by what I have already said. Above all, can it be asserted that any trait which Charles Dickens shares with his contemporaries is a significant feature of *Dickensian* style? Must not style be understood as a deviation from usual practice, the individual writer's way of choosing among available options? Here there are two answers to be given: a theoretical one and a practical one.

The theoretical answer involves a division of stylistics into two kinds. The first is reconstructive stylistics: its aim is to discover how a given author's linguistic choices would have struck a contemporary audience. A practitioner might take as his goal, for example, the description of a well-read seventeenth-century Englishman's response to the language of *Paradise Lost*. Reconstructive stylistics is at once impossible and indispensable. We can never know quite what it was to read *Paradise Lost* in the seventeenth century, and yet we cannot begin to think about *Paradise Lost* intelligently until we've tried to recreate such a reading. The other kind of study may be called subjective stylistics: it puts the language of *Paradise Lost* not only against the language of other works known to Milton's contemporaries but against the language of later works; it will set the linguistic figure of *Paradise Lost* against the linguistic ground of *The Prelude*. Considered in one way, this second stylistics is a special application of Eliot's famous theory:

> What happens when a new work of art is created is something that happens simultaneously to all the works of art which preceded it. . . . The existing order is complete before the new work arrives; for order to persist after the supervention of novelty, the *whole* existing order must be, if ever so slightly, altered; and so the relations, proportions, values of each work of art toward the whole are re-adjusted; and this is conformity between the old and the new. Whoever has approved this idea of order, of the form of European, of English literature, will not find it preposterous that the past should be altered by the present as much as the present is directed by the past.[3]

In the terms I've been using, each new sort of writing we know provides a ground against which we can—and at some time or other do—look at every other sort of writing we know. We are untrue to our own experience of Dickens if we silently pass by some feature of his language that is rarely encountered in later novelists but is common in Thackeray. And I would add that here, where language is concerned, to be untrue to our own experience is to miss important truths about Dickens. This would appear to be so, at any rate, if we take a semi-Whorfian position (as I do) and assume first that the linguistic habits of a writer not only express but also shape his meaning, and second, that the linguistic habits which most significantly shape a writer's meaning include those which neither the writer himself nor his contemporaries thought of as habits, peculiarities, at all; things which may strike us as mannerisms but to them were standard, neutral usages. One thing temporal separation gives us is a sense that what once seemed an inevitable or unremarkable usage is not that but in one respect or another "loaded" language. There are respects in which we shall never understand Dickens's language as well as a Victorian did; in other respects we may discover more in it than any Victorian could: we can never quite turn ourselves into natives of another period, but we can take advantage of the ways in which the true natives must inevitably be provincial while we are cosmopolitan. Alfred North Whitehead suggested that the most influential ideas of a given age were not the ones being debated at the time but the ones not discussed—the ideas taken for granted by everyone.[4] As with ideas, so with locutions.

That would be my theoretical answer to the question about methodology I have raised. It is an answer which in fact I do give here because what I am calling subjective stylistics is rich with possibilities for the bold investigator. But happily enough I myself need not be too bold just now. There is also a preactical answer to the question about methodology, and this is that Dickens does appear to use the suspended quotation (that still undefined device we are going to study) considerably more often than most other important novelists of the 1840s.[5] Since no one would want to define a writer's style as consisting of features which are used by that writer and *never* by other writers—since we all think of individual style as a matter of *frequency* of occurrence—the suspended quotation is a trait of Dickensian style worthy of investigation by practitioners of reconstructive stylistics, and we shall investigate it—putting aside, for now, the interesting fact that the suspended quotation is used far more by many novelists of the 1840s than it is by most novelists of the 1940s.

In a moment I am going to leave the suspended quotation proper for a time in order to look at its stylistic context. Before doing that, however, I ought to provide a usable definition: "suspended quotation" means a protracted interruption by the narrator of a character's speech. And here, "protracted" means containing at least five words. If asked why five rather than four or six, I can say only that this seems to me intuitively correct: to my ear a five-word interruption is usually intrusive and most of the time a four-word interruption is not. If asked why my working definition is based on number of words rather than number of syllables—that is, why I elect to treat "said Joe" as it if were the same size as "replied Pumblechook"—I can say only that I do so for the sake of convenience. I guess that I can sort out my plankton well enough with a comparatively coarse filter. Should I discover that the filter is too coarse—that is, if I keep finding that word-counts show no differences between passages where I hear differences—then I will do the work over again with a finer filter. (If the finer filter doesn't work, I will test some other variable. I never decide that I only *thought* I heard a difference and there really isn't one—though of course I hope that counting this and that will help me to hear differences that I hadn't heard before.)

As the first sentence of my epigraph would suggest, the suspended quotation has a particularly close association with the medial speech-tag—"said he," "answered Mrs. Worthington," "returned the Captain," etc.; more generally, one observes that the suspended quotation lives its vigorous nineteenth-century life surrounded by, competing, or combining with various other sorts of direct quotation and tags of different kinds. They are (for some of us!) fascinating, those sorts, those kinds, and I want to begin this study with a partial inventory of those stylistic options, adjust the microscope to 10X magnification for a while before turning it to 100X and thus restricting the field of vision ten times more. But as we start—even before we start—to look at this set of slides, let us have a noisy disruption. Into the lab comes commonsensical, ampersandriacal H. W. Fowler telling us not to squint into those nasty machines but to go out into the sunlight—advice which I'm sure many good writers would think quite salutary:

> Novelists and others who have to use dialogue as an ingredient in narrative are some of them unduly worried by the machinery problem. Tired of writing down *he said* & *said he* & *she replied* as often as they must, they

> mistakenly suppose the good old forms to be as tiring to their readers as to themselves, & seek relief in whimsical variations. The fact is that readers care what is said, but the frame into which a remark or a speech is fitted is indifferent to them; or rather, the virtue of frames is not that they should be various, but that they should be inconspicuous. It is true that an absolutely unrelieved monotony will itself become conspicuous; but the variety necessary to obviate that should be strictly limited to forms inconspicuous in themselves.[6]

There is something wholesome and hearty about that, certainly; but the fascinating thing about what Fowler calls *frames* and I call *tags* is that the variety of these available to the Victorian novelist and the variety of possibilities for their deployment and for the deployment of direct quotations themselves are far larger than would be needed simply to avoid monotony—and this is true after one has discarded all conspicuous, whimsical variations. "The fact is that readers care what is said, but the frame into which a remark or a speech is fitted is indifferent to them": most readers would agree, most Victorian novelists no doubt would have agreed—how remarkable, then, that inconspicuous forms should be so various, that there should have been such a senseless expenditure of writerly effort!

First of all, the nineteenth-century novelist has the option of withdrawing into pure drama: that is, he can simply start putting speech-prefixes before words spoken by his characters—for all the world as if he were writing for the stage. Thus, for instance, Peacock (who is very fond of this procedure) in *Nightmare Abbey:*

> *Marionetta.* I assure you, Mr. Flosky, I care no more about metaphysics than I do about the bank; and if you will condescend to talk to a simple girl in intelligible terms—
>
> *Mr. Flosky.* Say not condescend! Know you not that you talk to the most humble of men, to one who has buckled on the armour of sanctity, and clothed himself with humility as with a garment?

*Marionetta.* My cousin Scythrop has of late had an air of mystery about him, which gives me great uneasiness.
[chap. 8, p. 49]

Thackeray will insert scripts complete with stage directions into his novels, as, for instance, in book 2, chapter 9 of *The Newcomes*, and Surtees is quite willing to use speech-prefixes:

*Jorrocks.* The deuce! I forgot all that—curse Mrs. J—— and the Commons too. Well, Mr. Yorkshireman, I don't care if I do go with you—but where shall it be to? Some place where we can be quiet, for I really am werry bad, and not up to nothing like a lark.

*Yorkshireman.* Suppose we take a sniff of the briny—Margate—Ramsgate—Broadstairs?
[*Jorrocks' Jaunts and Jollities*, chap. 13, p. 239]

Such dramas within narratives had in their future the glory of the Nighttown chapter in *Ulysses* and in their past the different glory of *Pilgrim's Progress* (as well as, for example, chapter 8 of Fielding's *Jonathan Wild*). But on the whole, although the Victorian novelists are surely aware of the use of speech-prefixes and true stage directions in earlier and contemporary narratives, most of these authors do not lapse into genuine drama. There would seem to be a sense that no matter how economical scriptwriting conventions may be, these conventions carry one beyond the rules of the game, rules which seem to require that dialogue be contained within a narrative framework. The framework can be bent in many ways, but to insert a script is, for most Victorian tastes, not to bend but to break. Dickens will say "every writer of fiction, though he may not adopt the dramatic form, writes in effect for the stage,"[7] but when he is telling a story he is by God *telling* a story. This will be worth remembering.

Let us now move to those options which are exercised, with greater or lesser frequency, by virtually all Victorian novelists. Following Fowler's lead, I will consider the tag—the identifying unit which contains (in its most common, grammatically active form) a subject and a finite form of a transitive verb, the direct object of which is the quoted speech.[8] This identifying tag is felt to be "normally" present in Victorian direct quotations, but one of the most striking things about nineteenth-century novelists here, when they are compared with writers of the mid-eighteenth century and of many other periods, is that the Victorian storytellers are quite free to leave many speeches untagged and to give us such passages as:

> "Whose house is it?"
> "Mr. Rochester's."
> "Do you know Mr. Rochester?"
> "No, I have never seen him."
>
> [*Jane Eyre*, chap. 12, p. 100]

There are nineteenth-century novels in which this variation seems to occur more frequently than the "normal," tagged form of quotation: *Jane Eyre* is one example and Kingsley's *Yeast* is another.

Untagged quotations of the sort we find in this little exchange from *Jane Eyre* form a nice, clear, black/white contrast with tagged quotations. But there are also various shades of gray in nineteenth-century fiction. That is, a good many writers of this period are quite ingenious—inconspicuously ingenious—in finding ways to call our attention to a character who is *about* to speak, without actually saying that the following words, the ones bounded by quotation marks, were in fact spoken by that character. A suitably Victorian name for such practices would be "hints." Consider, for instance, this exchange from James's *Portrait of a Lady.* All three possibilities are here: we are taken from tag to hint to untagged speech; from black to gray to white:

> "Isabel will enjoy puzzling a lord," Mrs. Touchett remarked.
>
> Her son frowned a little. "What does she know about lords?"
>
> "Nothing at all: that will puzzle him all the more."
>
> [chap. 5, p. 58]

With these three possibilities in mind, we may start to ask some new questions about tagging, try to go beyond Fowler's hearty common sense. Let us draw an analogy from metrics. (In fact the present chapter might be considered an introduction to the metrics of quotation.) In iambic verse one is allowed to substitute a trochee for the first foot; such a substitution obviously has the negative function of preventing the hearer from becoming bored with too much of the same thing. In this sense, the initial trochee does for meter what Fowler wants inconspicuous variations in tagging to do for quotation. But those initial trochees, though they may sometimes have no more than this negative virtue of breaking up an overly regular pattern, often enough have a positive function as well: the trochee, the reversed first foot, tends to suggest a sudden spurt of energy, an extra push, and a poet who knows what he's doing will exploit the positive as well as the negative virtues of the trochee. In iambic verse the energizing trochee and the retarding spondee have the same negative function but quite different positive functions, and a good poet is not one for whom the choice of trochee or spondee is a matter of indifference.

Now if the tagged quotation is taken as the norm in nineteenth-century fiction, one may ask whether the choice of hint or untagged quotation is a matter of indifference, whether these variations have only the shared negative virtue of preventing a conspicuous sameness. Needless to say, I think the different variations do indeed have different positive functions and affect the reader in different ways. The untagged quotation speeds things up; it is a form of syncopation. It also leaves the reader rather more on his own than does the tagged quotation. The hint also leaves the reader on his own but draws attention to the fact that the reader is being left on his own; oddly, though the hint in fact provides the reader with more guidance than does the untagged quotation, it seems less courteous, more teasing. That is, the untagged quotation is normally used when paragraphing and context tell us all we must know to follow an exchange of speeches: the narrator is not needed, assumes in Fowleresque fashion, that we are simply interested in what is being said, and leaves us with the speeches themselves. With the hint the narrator swallows a camel and strains at a gnat (anyway, swallows a cake and strains at a cookie): he has slowed up the exchange of speeches in order to tell us something which often takes more time to tell than a normative tag would occupy. Furthermore, the hint form usually requires a longish pause (indicated here by James's full stop) between the hint and the following speech; the tag, which is part of the same sentence as the quoted words, does not require such an emphatic pause. All in all, the hint-quotation draws attention to the fact that something is being held back, that the reader is being made to figure something out for himself. Along with metrical analogies, here one might think of that venerable comparison in art history between the effects of a nude figure and those of a figure scantily, revealingly clad. In the *Jane Eyre* sort of untagged quotation there is naked dialogue: paragraphing and punctuation tell us what we must know, and that is that. The hint paragraph has a sort of mannerist, peekaboo effect, "her son frowned a little," seeming a veiled view of "her son frowned a little and said." If Rosa Dartle had written novels, she'd have liked this form of quotation very much indeed. (Rosa Dartle would have liked Henry James very much indeed.)

I spoke earlier of the hint-quotation as a gray between the black and white of tagged and untagged quotations. We may now look at the hint more closely and begin to discriminate among shades of gray. There are a good many ways in which these shadings may be ordered, but the ordering which is potentially most useful is probably one based on the closeness of the action described in the hint to the speech itself. The palest sort of hint would be that in which the action (or state) described has no particular association with speaking—for example, something like:

> George was standing near the door. "Now that really is preposterous."

At the other extreme, the hint might describe something

which is in fact the opening of a speech but must, because of the limits of our notational system, be placed outside quotation marks, described rather than directly quoted:

> George giggled. "Now that really is preposterous."

In between the two extremes come various sorts of body language, the facial varieties being the more emphatic hints:

> George rapped the table impatiently. "Now that really is preposterous."
>
> George smirked. "Now that really is preposterous."

Or indeed:

> Her son frowned a little. "What does she know about lords?"

The hint which is closest to the tag proper is that in which the novelist in fact tells us that a character *does* speak, but leaves us to infer that the quotation following this announcement is the speech in question. Thus Dickens's use of *catch her up* in an exchange from *Our Mutual Friend:*

> "Then you have not been to sea lately?"
> "No. Been in the sick bay since then, and been employed ashore."
> "Then, to be sure, that accounts for your hands."
> The man with a keen look, a quick smile, and a change of manner, caught her up. "You're a good observer. Yes. That accounts for my hands."
>
> [II, chap. 12, p. 353]

And thus *speaks* in this passage from *The Mystery of Edwin Drood:*

> Always kindly, but moved to be unusually kind this evening, and having bestowed kind words on most of the children and aged people he has met, he at once bends down, and speaks to this woman.
> "Are you ill?"
>
> [chap. 14, p. 161]

Substitute *says* for *speaks*, use a comma in place of a full stop, and this is a tagged quotation. Leave it as it is and there is a touch of the mysterious, something tense, about the passage. Another device very like this one in its tense laconism is one which I have in fact myself used in my last two citations: the use of *thus* rather than a speech-tag:

> "It is very high; it is a little difficult. Better to begin slowly." Thus, Monsieur Defarge, in a stern voice, to Mr. Lorry, as they began ascending the stairs.
>
> [*TTC*, I, chap. 5, p. 33]

The laconic air of this passage does not result from any genuine compression: it would be easy enough to make the speech attribution here explicit without adding one syllable to the length of the paragraph:

> "It is very high," said Monsieur Defarge in a stern voice to Mr. Lorry, as they began ascending the stairs. "It is a little difficult. Better to begin slowly."

So far I have been taking the tagged quotation—the quotation which is the direct object of a narrative verb—as the norm, analogous to the iambic foot in iambic verse. But just as the normal iambic foot may be subdivided into several different varieties with different degrees of contrast between the "unstressed" first syllable and the "stressed" second, so the normative tagged quotation comes in several varieties. Here the principal difference is of course where the tag is placed: before the quoted words, after them, or as an *inquit* between them (for example, " 'Yes,' he said, 'this is a splendid morning.' "). About this tripart division I shall have a good deal more to say later. For now, though, let me go on to another area of choice: the transitive verb to be used in a particular tag and the set of transitive verbs to be used frequently in a particular work.

It will simplify things considerably to begin by granting Fowler his point and exclude from consideration all highly conspicuous, precious, and even writer's-workshop-vivid choices (" 'Never!' he snarled, gasped, mumbled, growled, roared.”). I do this excluding both because I want to concentrate on less conspicuous features of style and also because I am interested not in unusual words which label unusual speech-acts but rather in high-frequency tag-verbs which by their very frequency of occurrence form a model of human speech within a particular novel, oeuvre, or period—give us, that is, our sense of what the main subvarieties, contrasting types of human utterance are.

What I am suggesting here is that one might profitably treat the set of high-frequency tag-verbs encountered in a particular novel, novelist, or age as what is called a “semantic field.” Such semantic fields (also referred to as “linguistic fields”) may be thought of, to quote Stephen Ullmann, as

> closely-knit sectors of the vocabulary, in which a particular [conceptual] sphere is divided up, classified and organized in such away that each element helps to delimit its neighbors and is delimited by them. . . . In each field, the raw material of experience is analyzed and elaborated in a unique way, differing from one language to another and often from one period to another in the history of the same idiom. In this way, the structure of semantic fields embodies a specific philosophy and a scale of values.[9]

Generally, semantic field analysis has not been of much practical value in the study of postmedieval texts; it is not an easy technique to use when there are more than a few subsections of each field. But tag-verbs (once we are willing to restrict ourselves to high-frequency forms) offer both a manageable and an interesting area for investigation.

Let us see how we might proceed, what questions we would ask. Though most semantic field theorists find quantitative considerations irrelevant, I suggest that one not only start with a quantitative entrance requirement and look only at high-frequency tag-verbs (those that are used, let us say, for at least 10 percent of the tagged quotations in a given sample), but that one continue to study quantity as the analysis proceeds. In Victorian fiction it will be found, not too surprisingly, that *say* is a base form, occurring in

40 percent to 60 percent of the tags. *Say* will be the norm: colorless, neutral, unmarked.

Now even here there is one possibility for stylistic differentiation: a novel in which *say* is used in 40 percent of the tags has a different texture from a novel where *say* is used in 60 percent of the tags. But of course there are more things to notice. What are those other high-frequency tag-verbs; what, in a particular work, is a character likely to be doing to or with his quoted words when he is not merely *saying* them? To take one possible categorization here, we may make a binary division which will likely be relevant to all or almost all of the marked high-frequency verbs. On the one hand there are verbs like *cry* and *exclaim* which are "lyric," and emphasize the subjective quality of the utterance and the emotional matrix from which it came; others (for example, *reply*, *interrupt*, *return*, *continue*) are "dramatic," and stress the relation of what is uttered now to what has been uttered before—draw attention to the "objective" status of this utterance as part of a set of utterances. It would obviously be of some interest to compare the proportions of lyric and dramatic tag-verbs in different works; it would also be interesting to see how each of the two areas is subdivided in a particular work. We may notice, for instance, when studying dramatic tags, that Victorians are far more likely to inform us that utterance B was a *reply* or *return* than they are to specify that utterance A, which provoked it, was a question: they will likely use *say* rather than *ask* or *inquire*—for example:

> "What is the matter?" *said* Mr. Pickwick to the boy.
> "Nothing's the matter, sir," *replied* the boy, expanding his mouth to the whole breadth of his countenance.
> [*PP*, chap. 50, p. 688]

To speak of "ask" or "inquire" brings us to another possibility for stylistic analysis, another linguistic option. Is this writer's (or period's) set of high-frequency tag-verbs generally more formal than that other's? One may notice, for instance, that Dickens, in contrast to Fielding, shows a striking preference for the "literary" *reply* and *return* rather than the neutral *answer;* and to notice this is to notice something quite significant. When dealing with a skillful novel—a novel worth dealing with—it is at times difficult to find a choice which is purely and unambiguously a reflection of authorial style, preferred level of usage; where the choice of this rather than that expression involves on the one hand *only* a change in the level of usage and not in the nature of the referent, and on the other hand, is clearly not a response to some local occasion—the appearance of a character who provokes satiric or pathetic or solemn language. As an index to the style of a work or period, the use of *reply/return* rather than *answer* has no awkwardness or ambiguity about it. Such a choice is as purely a matter of linguistic level as one is likely to find. It is a choice made again and again. Dickens employs the more elegant forms in chapter after chapter, with all kinds of characters and all kinds of situations: one could hardly maintain that Dickens selects *reply/return* rather than *answer* because the more learned form is more expressive of what is happening *just here.* And finally, just because we are speaking about a high-frequency choice which does not obtrude itself upon the reader's attention, we are talking about just the sort of thing which gives the book (or oeuvre) as a whole its characteristic texture, air, tone. One would want to find further examples, of course, but it seems to me that the difference between Fielding's practice and Dickens's in the use of this one sort of tag-verb is not likely to be a "freak case": almost certainly we will find, by whatever other tests we use, that the normative narrational diction of *Dombey and Son* is more formal than that of *Tom Jones.*

We will notice that certain tag-verbs have strange eventful histories, are studies in themselves. *Cry* is probably the most important of these words. If one looks at tags in *The Vicar of Wakefield*, for instance, one notices that there the *cry* is one of the principal forms of human utterance:

> —"What signifies minding her," cried the host, "if she be slow, she is sure."—"I don't know that," replied the wife; "but I know that I am sure she has been here a fortnight, and

we have not yet seen the cross of her money."—"I suppose, my dear," cried he, "we shall have it all in a lump."—"In a lump!" cried the other, "I hope we may get it any way; and that I am resolved we shall this very night, or out she tramps, bag and baggage."—"Consider, my dear," cried the husband, "she is a gentlewoman, and deserves more respect."

[chap. 21][10]

Undoubtedly *cry* becomes less important as we move into the nineteenth century and then on to the twentieth: but this decline is not steady and wants analysis. One would like to know, of course, which nineteenth-century novelists retain a taste for *cry*; but one would also like to know where the decibel level of novelistic conversation really becomes lower and where *cry* is simply displaced by more learned synonyms (*exclaim*, *ejaculate*).

One thing we usually do not talk about in discussing fiction but which is, in fact, of considerable stylistic interest is page layout and punctuation. These things do change and the passage I've just quoted from *The Vicar of Wakefield* has a somewhat odd look to it. If we think about the matter for a moment, we realize that in a nineteenth- or twentieth-century novel Goldsmith's series of words would almost certainly have been broken up into a number of different paragraphs, a new one coming with every change of speaker. Later in this book I shall be talking about some of the effects these new layout conventions (the ones generally accepted by Dickens's time and partially violated by Goldsmith) have upon the reading and writing of fictional dialogue. Here, though, I will at least assert that the new rules for the presentation of dialogue—that is

1. A new speaker is given a new paragraph

and also

2. Quotation marks are to be placed around utterances recorded with word for word accuracy

—testify to a sense of the importance and dignity of the spoken word. (Rule 1 is the novelistic equivalent of "the labourer is worthy of his hire," and a new voice now deserves something more than a Goldsmithian dash; rule 2 insists that it is not enough for the reader to learn from punctuation that there is quoting in this part of the text: punctuation must show the reader precisely what is quoted from each speaker.)[11] But the main point I want to make right here about these new rules is that they are not, in the period which concerns us, quite as inevitably obeyed as, for example, the rules for capitalizing proper names—and of course a rule which is not always obeyed—an "optional rule," so to speak—is a matter of style. Let me be specific. First of all, as Dickens is beginning his career, the older sort of paragraphing is not entirely obsolete. *Pickwick Papers*, as most introductions will inform us, was to some extent stimulated into existence by the popularity of Surtees's *Jorrocks' Jaunts and Jollities;* and in *Jorrocks* dialogue is frequently presented in the old way:

> The man eyed him with a mixed look of incredulity and contempt. At length, putting his thumbs into the armholes of his waistcoat, he replied, "I bet a crown you know as well as I do." "Done," said Mr. Jorrocks holding out his hand. "No—I won't do that," replied the man, "but I'll tell you what I'll do with you,—I'll lay you two to one, in fives or fifties if you like, that you knew before you axed, and that Thunderbolt don't win the Riddlesworth." "Really," said Mr. Jorrocks, "I'm not a betting man." "Then, wot the 'ell business have you at Newmarket?" was all the answer he got.
>
> [chap. 5, p. 81]

Thus it seems quite legitimate (though perhaps not of great utility) to say that in the first years of Dickens's career, the use of the new convention was a decision to mark the individuality of the speaking voice more rather than less elaborately. More important—at least for purposes of local explication, practical criticism—is the departure from the standard practice within a single work. In *Bleak House*, for instance, the new change-of-paragraph rule is followed; thus when we come to the following exchange

> Says the Coroner, is that boy here? Says the beadle, no, sir, he is not here. Says the Coroner, go and fetch him then. In the absence of the active and intelligent, the Coroner converses with Mr. Tulkinghorn.
>
> [chap. 11, p. 148]

we notice that an authorial contempt for the proceedings is suggested by the denial to the speakers of usual perquisites: not only a new paragraph for every new speech, but quotation marks to frame and guarantee the purity of a character's *ipsissima verba.* There is, of course, punctuational justice here: these characters are speaking "unnaturally," this is not true conversation but a ritualized, legalistic parody of a human conversation. Dickens, let us say, punishes the characters for their pseudointerchange by withholding the marks of true conversation.

*Bleak House* is of course notable for its experiments with various narrational and stylistic devices, and we should not be surprised to find that some of the experiments there involve the presentation of direct discourse. What is more surprising is the fact that we can find expressive violation of the paragraphing convention in such a work as Charles Kingsley's *Yeast*, a novel where message is all, and rather more than all. Notice how Kingsley treats the moment at which the character Tregarva, who appeared drowned, shows signs of life:

> "Carry him to the house," said the colonel, in a despairing tone, after another attempt.
>
> "He moves!" "No!" "He does!" "He breathes!" "Look at his eyelids!"
>
> [chap. 3, p. 68]

Here, obviously, the failure to give each exclamation a territory of its own creates the impression of a rush of comments, an overlapping of speeches. Obviously, I say; and this obviousness may be most notable here: awareness of the new rule as *a* rule, not quite inviolable, and responsiveness to the effects to be obtained through violation of that rule are certainly not coterie things for the Victorians.

The *Yeast* and *Bleak House* passages show us direct discourse being presented, momentarily, without normal ceremoniousness. In both passages the absence of the usual author-to-character courtesies proves quite easy to interpret, and this will, in fact, almost always be the case when such perquisites are withheld. More often puzzling, at least for the twentieth-century reader of Victorian fiction, is the book where we come upon the opposite situation: the according of these perquisites to passages which are not directly quoted. I turn to Surtees and Jorrocks once again, though this time my selection comes from *Handley Cross* rather than the *Jaunts and Jollities.* One finds here not a violation of the modern rule for paragraphing but a violation of the quotation mark rule—here those marks are being used for indirect rather than direct quotation:

> "Duke," she said, "was unfortunately at that moment with some important justice business"—(decanting the wine).
> Mr. Jorrocks "'Oped his grace wouldn't 'urry himself."
> "It was very provoking," she continued, without regarding Mr. Jorrocks' observation; "but the whole county came to him for justice, and Duke could hardly be said to have a moment to himself."
>
> [chap. 34, p. 310]

We find that in his liking for this practice Thackeray is more like Surtees than like Dickens. Notice how quotation marks are employed in the following passage from *Vanity Fair.* They distinguish not between direct speech and everything else but between on the one hand "everything else" and on the other both direct quotation and *all-but-direct* quotation: if a passage differs from a character's *ipsissima verba* merely in the use of past tense rather than present and the substitution of one pronoun for another (that is, *was* for *is; should he* for *shall I*), it may be put in quotation marks; if there are more complex editorial substitutions (for example, *had Captain Dobbin* for [*Captain Dobbin*(?)], *have you; that day* for *today*), it may not:[12]

The fact is, when Captain Dobbin blushed so, and looked

> so awkward, he remembered a circumstance of which he did not think it was necessary to inform the young ladies, viz., that he had been calling at Mr. Sedley's house already, on the pretence of seeing George, of course, and George wasn't there, only poor little Amelia, with rather a sad wistful face, seated near the drawing-room window, who, after some very trifling stupid talk, ventured to ask, *was* there any truth in the report that the regiment *was* soon to be ordered abroad; and *had Captain Dobbin* seen *Mr. Osborne that day?*
>
> The regiment *was* not ordered abroad as yet; and *Captain Dobbin had* not seen George. "He *was* with his sister, most likely," the Captain said. "*Should he* go and fetch the truant?" So she gave him her hand kindly and gratefully: and he crossed the square; and she waited and waited, but George never came.
>
> [*Vanity Fair*, chap. 12, I.132–33. Italics added]

Historically, this is a continuation of eighteenth-century practice;[13] Surtees, Thackeray, and, for example, Austen and Scott before them, are more "conservative" than Dickens in this respect. But what is historically more conservative is, arguably, the reflection of a more casual attitude toward the spoken word. In the older convention, one marks off as all one thing both *ipsissima verba* quotations and also quotations in which there are a few easily recognizable substitutions: *de minimis non curat lex.*[14] Under the new dispensation, quotation marks certify that there has been no tinkering with tenses or pronouns. What we have here, of course, is not primarily a pair of techniques to be chosen between according to the local effects one wants in a particular chapter, but rather a lifelong choice of the older broad constructionist convention or the newer strict constructionism. Whichever choice a Victorian writer makes, he and his readers know works which follow the other convention. (Thackeray's may be the minority choice, but everyone read Thackeray!) Thus we must recognize that when Dickens uses quotation marks in what seems to us a normal way, that normal usage represents a stylistic choice, and that stylistic choice, in turn, reflects a choice between two attitudes toward the integrity of speech. (We may differ about the best way to describe the implications of the choice, but ought to agree that the choice exists and has something to do with an author's attitude toward the speech of his characters.)

Finally, one might notice that the broad constructionist writer may occasionally fall into the medieval habit of using mixed forms of discourse: switching quite abruptly from indirect to direct quotation, as in this passage from Thackeray's *Pendennis:*

> Pen, with a laugh, said "that at one time he did think he [Pen himself] was pretty well in Miss Amory's good graces. But my mother did not like her, and the affair went off." Pen did not think it fit to tell his uncle all the particulars of the courtship which had passed between himself and the young lady.
>
> [II.2, p. 22. Bracketed phrase added]

Such a change of construction is consistent with the attitude which uses quotation marks in the older way: a broad constructionist writer does not have the strict constructionist's perception that a directly quoted speech is different in kind from speeches which have been subjected to any lexical or syntactic modification. Thackeray wanders across a county line; for Dickens, for most of us, that county line is an international frontier.[15]

An international frontier, yes; but it is, let us say, a frontier which matters far more to those on one side of the boundary than to those on the other: the absence of quotation marks in a passage about a character's thoughts or statements ordinarily guarantees nothing *except that the passage is not an absolutely pure transcription of those thoughts or statements.* Such a passage may, for instance, contain only such words and constructions as the narrator of the work would himself judge seemly; or it may, on the other hand, contain peculiarities of diction and syntax which one associates with the character and not the narrator. (The device used in this second kind of passage is called *erlebte Rede* or *style indirect libre.*)[16] The concern for purity is a concern for the purity of the material within the strict constructionist's quotation marks: dialogue (and this will prove to be a matter of considerable importance later in this study) dialogue is the more prestigious, rich, attractive land: it allows emigration, but not immigration.

Knowing the superior attractiveness of direct quotation within the work, a nineteenth-century novelist will achieve a variety of effects by using direct quotation for some parts of a conversation but not others. One may call to mind both an extreme and very common form of mixture: there will be a question directly quoted, and the reply put not only in indirect quotation but in a diction far removed from any the character would employ. The legalistic/journalistic "in the affirmative" is a particular favorite:

> "Why if I felt less like a walking brandy-bottle, I shouldn't be quite so staggery this mornin'," replied Sam. "Are you stoppin' in this house, old 'un?"
> The mulberry man replied in the affirmative.
> [*PP*, chap. 16, pp. 212–13]

> After reflecting about it, with a sagacious air, Mr. Barkis eyed her, and said:
> "*Are* you pretty comfortable?"
> Peggotty laughed, and answered in the affirmative.
> [*DC*, chap. 10, p. 137]

Such high-handedness on the author's part—the sudden denial to one character of the privilege just accorded another, the use of grotesquely improbable diction in the paraphrase to make the inequality of treatment all the more striking—is a sort of affectionate teasing when the victim is someone like Peggotty; but elsewhere the device suggests a real contempt: why bother with what such a character as *this* would actually say here?

> "Don't let me detain you, Mr. Wegg. I'm not company for any one."
> "It's not on that account," says Silas, rising, "but because I've got an appointment. It's time I was at Harmon's."
> "Eh?" said Mr. Venus. "Harmon's, up Battle Bridge way?"
> *Mr. Wegg admits he is bound for that port.*

"You ought to be in a good thing, if you've worked yourself in there. There's lots of money going there."

[*OMF*, I.VII, p. 84. Italics added]

Elsewhere there are subtler uses. The effect of the following passage from *Little Dorrit* depends not at all upon grotesquely improbable paraphrase; rather Dickens exploits just that distinction between forms of quotation which matters to strict constructionists but not to broad constructionists. The topic of conversation here is mountains:

"But you are familiar with them, sir?" the insinuating traveller assumed.

"I am—hum—tolerably familiar. Not of late years. Not of late years," replied the Chief, with a flourish of his hand.

The insinuating traveller, acknowledging the flourish with an inclination of his head, passed from the Chief to the second young lady, who had not yet been referred to, otherwise than as one of the ladies in whose behalf he felt so sensitive an interest.

*He hoped she was not incommoded by the fatigues of the day.*

"Incommoded, certainly," returned the young lady, "but not tired."

The insinuating traveller complimented her on the justice of the distinction. It was what he had meant to say. Every lady must doubtless be incommoded, by having to do with that proverbially unaccommodating animal, the mule.

"We have had, of course," said the young lady, who was rather reserved and haughty, "to leave the carriages and fourgon at Martigny. And the impossibility of bringing anything that one wants to that inaccessible place, and the necessity of leaving every comfort behind, is not convenient."

"A savage place, indeed," said the insinuating traveller.

[II, 1.435. Italics added]

Consider the exquisite maliciousness of that italicized sentence. For the old dispensation novelist, as I have said, a quotation which seems so lightly altered would be within the pale: if one can write,

> Mr. Jorrocks "'Oped his grace wouldn't 'urry himself."

one can also write—*would* also write,

> He "hoped she was not incommoded by the fatigues of the day."

Dickens, the new-dispensation novelist, grants it some of the perquisites of the direct quotation it *almost* is: the Dickensian sentence is given a paragraph to itself, though in fact in its present, indirect form it might quite easily have been attached to the previous paragraph. But Dickens *will* keep Rigaud, for a time, to the tense and pronouns of indirect quotation, and outside quotation marks; castigates Rigaud by granting him, for the moment, *all but* the privileges of his interlocutors; refuses, in an exchange which turns upon imagined verbal distinctions, to guarantee that he has presented Rigaud's diction as accurately as he had recorded the diction of the other characters. Or perhaps, in the present case, we might want to analyze the effect in another way. We know that Rigaud is, after all, not quite conversing with these people; he is milking information from them. Their utterances are, at least when compared with his, artless, real. Perhaps that more complex sort of manipulation one finds in his speech is both reflected and punished by the indirect form of quotation to which Rigaud is momentarily confined.

Let us keep Rigaud's milking of information in mind as we consider this passage from *A Tale of Two Cities:*

> Jacques One struck in, and asked if he had ever seen the man before?
>
> "Never," answered the mender of roads, recovering his perpendicular.
>
> Jacques Three demanded how he afterwards recognized him then?
>
> "By his tall figure," said the mender of roads, softly, and with his finger at his nose. "When Monsieur the Marquis

demands that evening, 'Say, what is he like?' I make response, 'Tall as a spectre.'"

"You should have said, short as a dwarf," returned Jacques Two.

[II, chap. 15, p. 159]

Here there is nothing punitive about the nonce assignment of indirect discourse to some characters and direct discourse to others; the use of different forms is more simply a way of directing (or reflecting) our attention. The use of two different forms of quotation in a single conversation readily—inevitably—suggests visual analogies. The directly quoted character is placed in a brighter light than the indirectly quoted character; or, in a cinematic translation of the passage just quoted, Jacques One and Jacques Three might have either their backs or profiles to the camera, while Jacques Two and the mender of roads would be photographed full-face—or perhaps the mender of roads and Jacques Two would be presented in close-up, and the indirectly quoted characters seen in long shots.[17]

Obviously enough, freedom to construct a conversation out of two kinds of quotations, direct and indirect, allows the novelist to reinforce or create distinctions of a great many kinds—quite as many as a film director can with two contrasting shots. One will find it more than instructive to analyze mixtures of direct and indirect quotations in late Dickensian conversations, for instance; particularly with longer exchanges, one will notice intricate rhythms being created or enhanced through the varying assignments of indirect quotation/direct quotation to character one/character two/character three, etc. But though the binary opposition of direct and indirect quotation is variously useful and readily analyzed, it is obviously not the only sort of contrast which can be used in presenting conversations. "Indirect quotation" is itself more than one thing; the term covers a number of forms in which different sorts of liberties are taken with the character's original wording. Now, however, I shall do no more than mention that particular complexity, for *erlebte Rede* has been much studied, and my interest here is not in indirect quotation per se but in indirect quotation when it is part of the environment of direct quotation. We consider direct quotation itself, then, and realize that the various sorts of tags touched on in this chapter can be contrasted with one another to create various subtle effects. But we also realize that one form of contrast between different direct quotations—that contrast between tagged and untagged quotations which we spoke of early in this chapter in terms of novelistic metrics—can be used to draw the reader's attention more to one character than another in a particular conversation or part of a conversation. Basically, the directive signals given by the set untagged/tagged are like those given by the set indirect quotation/direct quotation, but are somewhat subtler, less emphatic, than the latter. The Victorians will often use that subtler (and less invidious) tagged/untagged contrast for parts of conversations in which a sympathetic and dignified character has a comic or at least colorful interlocutor—in which the dignified character, as the straight man, is given untagged speeches and the colorful character tagged ones. (Fancy tags some of them; others quite plain.) Thus, from Dickens's last book, this section of a conversation between Septimus and his mother. The first speech is by Septimus:

> "Well! Mr. Neville, on that unfortunate occasion, commits himself under provocation."
>
> "And under mulled wine," *added the old lady.*
>
> "I must admit the wine. Though I believe the two young men were much alike in that regard."
>
> "I don't," *said the old lady.*
>
> "Why not, Ma?"
>
> "Because I *don't*," *said the old lady.* "Still, I am quite open to discussion."
>
> "But my dear Ma, I cannot see how we are to discuss, if you take that line."
>
> "Blame Mr. Neville for it, Sept, and not me," *said the old lady, with stately severity.*
>
> "My dear Ma! why Mr. Neville?"

> "Because," *said Mrs. Crisparkle, retiring on first principles*, "he came home intoxicated, and did great discredit to this house, and showed great disrespect to this family."
>
> [*ED*, chap. 10, p. 97. Italics added to tags]

There is a related ordering of the reader's attention in this bit of conversation from Disraeli's *Sybil:*

> "Well, do you know, Mr. Charles, between ourselves," *and Mr. Bingley lowered his tone, and looked about him*, "things is very bad here; I can't make out, for my part, what has become of the country. 'Tayn't the same land to live in as it was when you used to come to our moor coursing, with the old lord; you remember that, I be sure, Mr. Charles."
>
> "'Tis not easy to forget good sport, Mr. Bingley. With your permission, I will put my horse up here, for half an hour. I have a fancy to stroll the ruins."
>
> "You wunna find them much changed," *said the farmer, smiling.* "They have seen a deal of different things in their time! But you will taste our ale, Mr. Charles?"
>
> "When I return."
>
> [I.iv, p. 57]

Another interesting option for the Victorian novelist is to create a sense of distance between the speaker and his speech by using a tag which is syntactically or semantically passive, and makes speech rather than speaker the subject of the sentence, or shifts emphasis from the production of the speech to its perception. Such tags are highly conspicuous and not likely to occur hundreds of times in a single work; they may be employed to suggest, for example, Florence Dombey's timidity:

> "I should much prefer it, aunt," was the faint rejoinder.
>
> [chap. 18, p. 245]

Or for the odd gothic touch:

> By degrees, in the pauses of his quick and laboured breathing, he was heard to say:
>
> "What is this?"
>
> [*TTC*, I, chap. 6, p. 42]

"Commence," was Monsieur Defarge's not unreasonable reply, "at the commencement."

[*TTC*, II, chap. 15, p. 159]

With the Rigaud passage quoted earlier (p. 25) we might compare the following paragraphs from the same novel, in which the difference between the open Mr. Meagles and the reserved Miss Wade is emphasized by the contrast between the active tag-verb in his speech and the semantically passive tag inserted in hers:

"Good-bye!" said Mr. Meagles. "This is the last good-bye upon the list, for mother and I have just said it to Mr. Clennam here, and he only waits to say it to Pet. Good-bye! We may never meet again."

"In our course through life we shall meet the people who are coming to meet *us*, from many strange places and by many strange roads," was the reserved reply; "and what it is set to us to do to them, and what it is set to them to do to us, will all be done."

[*LD*, I, chap. 2, p. 25][18]

Besides an occasional passive, the Victorian novelist may use participial constructions in tags (most often *was saying* rather than *said.*) Generally the participial construction makes it seem that the audience of the novel (and perhaps the audience within the novel) just *happens* to hear this utterance. "Was saying" suggests that the tape recorder was left on by accident and these words were picked up, rather than that the tape recorder is deliberately employed to pick up just such utterances; "was saying" quotation may remind us a bit of voice overlap in the movies. An example from *Adam Bede:*

Mr. Poyser thought she looked the prettier for it: it was a flush no deeper than the petal of a monthly rose. Perhaps it came because her uncle was looking at her so fixedly; but there is no knowing; for just then Adam was saying, with quiet surprise,

"Why I hoped Dinah was settled among us for life. I

thought she'd given up the notion o' going back to her old country."

[chap. 59, p. 489]

Five pages earlier, in the third paragraph of the sixth book, Eliot had used the same construction. There it more obviously suggests that the speaker is rather the less interesting of the two characters who are going to engage in a duologue, and that the response to the speech tagged in this way will likely be more significant than this speech itself. (In other words, the initial participial works toward the same end as the association of untagged speeches with one of two characters engaged in a conversation.) Here the participially tagged speech is quoted verbatim, but the "was saying" makes it seem less detached from the preceding setting-of-scene than a simple preterite would:

> Totty is larger by more than two years' growth than when you first saw her, and she has on a black frock under her pinafore: Mrs. Poyser too has on a black gown, which seems to heighten the family likeness between her and Dinah. In other respects there is little outward change now discernible in our old friends, or in the pleasant house-place, bright with oak and pewter.
>
> "I never saw the like to you, Dinah," Mrs. Poyser was saying, "when once you've took anything into your head. . . ."
>
> [p. 484]

That last quotation, "'I never saw the like to you, Dinah,' Mrs. Poyser was saying" brings to mind another syntactical option worth attending to. One of the most remarked tendencies in the history of English is toward the more and more frequent employment of the syntactical order subject-verb-object, and especially the order subject-verb. Now with a tagged quotation of the most common sort, quoted words are of course the direct object of the sentence, the speaker the subject, and the tag-verb the main verb of the sentence. As we enter the period of the nineteenth- and twentieth-century novels, we find that an older, Germanic rule still governs the syntax of medially and finally tagged quotation: that is, when a sentence begins with the direct object, the verb must follow and the subject then come in the third position: [O-V-S(-O)]. Thus,

> "Beg your pardon, sir," *said Mrs. Craddock,* the landlady, peeping in; "but *did* you want anything more, sir?"
> "Nothing more, ma'am," *replied Mr. Pickwick.*
> [*PP*, chap. 36, p. 506]

On the other hand, when we have an initial tag—subject and verb preceding object—subject precedes verb [S-V-O]:

> The old gentleman having concluded his dictation, and Mr. Snodgrass having returned his note-book to his pocket, *Mr. Pickwick said:*
> "Excuse me, sir, for making the remark on so short an acquaintance; but . . . ."
> [*PP*, chap. 6, p. 73]

But the tendency to universalize the order S-V is making itself felt here, and one finds considerable variation in the syntax of Victorian tags. When compared with Dickens, Thackeray is notably informal, newfangled in his tagging; he freely employs the S-V order even when the sentence begins with the quoted words as object:

> "*I'll* make your fortune," *she said;* and Delilah patted Samson's cheek.
> "You can do anything," *he said,* kissing the little hand. "By Jove, you can; and we'll drive down to the Star and Garter, and dine, by Jove."
> [*Vanity Fair*, chap. 16, I.196]

If I examine one hundred consecutive medially or finally tagged quotations in *Vanity Fair* (starting with the first such quotation in chapter 17) I find that seventy-nine of the tags have S-V syntax and only twenty-one follow the older V-S pattern; with a like sample beginning with the seventeenth chapter of *Dombey and Son*, I find only two examples of the more colloquial O-S-V(-O) order and ninety-eight of the more formal O-V-S(-O) order. Though Thackeray doubtless employs V-S tags more frequently in some sections of his work than in others (this in itself would be an interesting subject for study) there can be no doubt that S-V/V-S usage is a valuable index to level of formality in different works from a given decade of the nineteenth or twentieth century: valuable because this choice can hardly reflect anything more than the writer's sense of the correct level of formality, and the choice is one which unobtrusively colors almost every page of a given novel.

Well, you see the possibilities. Or, let us say, you have already lost—temporarily—that sweet obliviousness to tags which you owed yesterday. Or, more exactly, you have temporarily lost your ability (always an imperfect one) to filter out those tags as you read along. Stop here, and you'll be quite your novel-reading self again in a day or two. Press on, and I think I can promise you a small but permanent shift in the way you perceive good nineteenth-century novels; or, again more exactly, in the way you perceive yourself perceiving those novels.

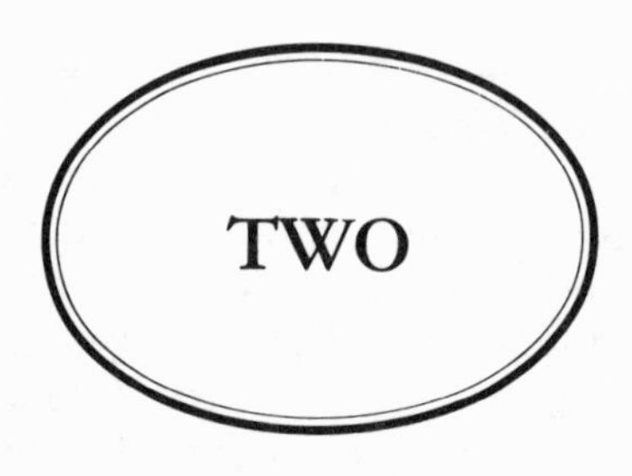

# The Suspended Quotation: Contexts and Interpretations

A few assumptions. For the nineteenth-century novelist, as we have seen, direct quotation is not a single option but a set of options: there are various ways to set out a character's *ipsissima verba*. And the way a novelist chooses among these options is expressive and meaningful, even if the novelist himself is not quite aware of that expressiveness. But meaningfulness, expressiveness—these are slippery notions. In the last quarter of the twentieth century one does not believe in single, correct interpretations of artistic works, and one believes even less (if possible) in correct interpretations of stylistic habits. It is true, though, that one has psychological needs as well as hermeneutic theories. We cannot become aware of an unusual pattern of choice in some novelist or poet, notice a strong taste for some verbal device, and not ask *why*-questions. We may even find that we require a single answer rather than a group of answers. It may prove impossible—it does for me—to notice a writer's exceptional liking for one particular device and believe that there is no underlying unity in that preference: that is, I am not content to conclude that an author uses a certain form with unusual frequency because that form just happens to lend itself to three different and unrelated sorts of effects, all three of which that writer just happens to like. What one does, given these various needs, is of course proceed as if it were possible to find definitive interpretations of stylistic preferences. One does this because it is so hard not to, and one does this in public—publishes interpretations—in large part because the attempt to "read" a stylistic mannerism (the hypothesizing, the making of analogies, the leaping from thing to thing, and seeking connections in unlikely places, and yes, the counting, the wretched counting) can bring pleasure to others. In any case, I hope the reason is in large part this!

Now the business at hand is an explanation of the heavy use of suspended quotations in the early novels of Charles Dickens. The process of explaining is much here, but it is not everything, and I should say a few words about results. It is, then, my hope that by the end of this study you will have not only an interpretation of what seems to me the most interesting of the stylistic habits mentioned in the previous chapter but: first, a new sense of the relationship established among Charles Dickens, his readers, and his characters; second, a changed awareness of what we ourselves do as we read along in a nineteenth-century English novel; third (and this, though it may not sound very attractive, is also worth having), a new understanding of what it was the old-fashioned Dickensians reacted to in those late Dickens novels which they found disappointing and modern critics consider masterpieces. As to my central concern: the heavy Dickensian use of suspended quotation seems to be fundamentally a sort of aggression. Though it serves many local purposes, seems at times almost embarrassingly overdetermined, the suspended quotation is most deeply an expression of hostility toward his own characters by an author who resents the special attractiveness those characters have for the audience. It is the resource of a jealous author. This does sound peculiar; but wait and see.

We start by moving in close and examining a moment in one of Dickens's most widely read novels, *Great Expectations.* What interests me is a speech made by Mrs. Joe in the chapter 15 forge scene. You will recall the context: there has been trouble because Dolge Orlick, the journeyman blacksmith, wants time off for himself if Pip is to have a half-holiday to visit with Miss Havisham. Mrs. Joe, as one might expect, *will* interfere, enters the forge where she does not belong, and soon Orlick is calling her a foul shrew. Intent on forcing her husband to avenge her, Mrs. Joe addresses first the journeyman and then Pip. She says:

> "What did you say? What did you say? What did that fellow Orlick say to me, Pip? What did he call me, with my husband standing by? O! O! O! What was the name that he gave me before the base man who swore to defend me? O! Hold me! O!"

And that is what Mrs. Joe *says*. But her words are strange to us as we read them in this form, because Dickens presents her speech in a different way: makes a suspended quotation out of it. Here, then, is Mrs. Joe's outburst as we actually experience it in the novel:

> "What did you say?" cried my sister, beginning to scream. "What did you say? What did that fellow Orlick say to me, Pip? What did he call me, with my husband standing by? O! O! O!" Each of these exclamations was a shriek; and I must remark of my sister, what is equally true of all the violent women I have ever seen, that passion was no excuse for her, because it is undeniable that instead of lapsing into passion, she consciously and deliberately took extraordinary pains to force herself into it, and became blindly furious by regular stages; "what was the name that he gave me before the base man who swore to defend me? O! Hold me! O!"
> [p. 107]

The direct quotation is broken into by the narrator so that he can tell us one thing or another about the context, value, or meaning of that speech.

Now a suspended quotation can be quite powerful, expressive, effective, in its immediate context: it is a handy gadget for the novelistic tool-kit. And clearly Dickens uses the gadget quite expertly in this paragraph. Here the reader is satisfied, senses that if not quite poetic justice, then at least rhetorical justice has been meted out to Pip's terrible sister. The flow of her speech is broken,[1] and thus Mrs. Joe's implicit claim to being swept away by an accelerating emotion becomes doubly ridiculous: while the content of the narrative interjection points out the falsity of the implicit claim, the placing of the interjection destroys the very rhythm which is the evidence for that claim. As narrator, Pip breaks a sequence of words which depends for its effect upon our sense of an irresistibly growing intensity of feeling, and in doing this he ruins for us (and shields us from) what is, for Mrs. Joe's intended audience, a highly effective performance. "Hold me!" says Mrs. Joe; and this is in one sense what Pip has already done.

This is what Pip has done—but the narrator here is only nominally (or, better, pronominally) distinct from the usual Dickensian narrator. "And I must remark of my sister, what is equally true of all the violent women I have ever seen. . . ." The maker of those phrases is urbane, coolly essayistic in his tone, and, quite clearly, experienced, having seen many violent women. (How nicely that polite "I *must* remark" comments upon the necessity which is the domestic tyrant's plea.) She is by no means an unworthy opponent, this Mrs. Joe Gargery: she has the raw stuff of a Cicero. And the Dickensian narrator uses every advantage he has to defeat her. He employs a far more prestigious diction than she commands, and his syntax is notably more elegant; and of course he, and not Mrs. Joe, controls this book: he can break in whenever he likes and shut her off for a moment or two. It is given to the later, narrating quasi-Pip to stop his sister's words here. But remember what follows in *Great Expectations*. It will soon be given to Pip's brutal double, Dolge Orlick, to stop her words permanently. Even before she utters it, Mrs. Joe's request, "Hold me!" has been fulfilled by the narrator; immediately after she makes her request, we read: "'Ah-h-h!' growled the journeyman between his teeth, 'I'd hold you, if you was my wife. I'd hold you under the pump and choke it out of you.'"

Having pointed these things out, one might go on to write a critical essay on the values, meaning, and tensions of *Great*

*Expectations*: which is to say, the particular suspended quotation just considered is so expressive within its context that the question of why Dickens uses this device seems quite adequately answered. And of course there are hundreds of other suspended quotations in Dickens which are locally interpretable, which can be satisfactorily justified by close reading. As to the presence of the gadget in the Dickensian toolbox—well, Dickens and his contemporaries were certainly not the inventors of the device or the first ones to see its possibilities. Consider Sterne, for instance; in fact, consider Sterne by all means, for surely Sterne was the first novelist to see what this thing might accomplish. I'll do with the famous first speech of poor Walter Shandy what I did with Mrs. Joe's words. Here, first, is an unedited transcript:

> "Good G--! Did ever woman, since the creation of the world, interrupt a man with such a silly question?"

And here is what Sterne actually places on the first page of *Tristram Shandy:*

> —*Good G--!* cried my father, making an exclamation, but taking care to moderate his voice at the same time, —*Did ever woman, since the creation of the world, interrupt a man with such a silly question?*

Woe to any English major who cannot write five pages about *that!* Form and content beautifully joined, the interruption of a protest about an interruption. There it is: self-reflexive *Tristram Shandy*, the most professable novel in the language.[2]

And it is not difficult to find suspended quotations after Sterne. Consider the following description of a visit to a dying parishioner (the appropriately named Mr. Cayenne) in Galt's *Annals of the Parish* (1821; written 1813):

> When I had been seated some time, the power was given him to raise his head as it were ajee, and he looked at me with the tail of his eye, which I saw was glittering and glassy. "Doctor," for he always called me doctor, though I am not

of that degree, "I am glad to see you," were his words, uttered with some difficulty.
[chap. 47, p. 191; *ajee* in this passage means "to one side"]

Galt is not a writer one associates with pyrotechnics, but clearly he is at home with the suspended quotation and able to use it in a way both original and charming. It is the Reverend Mr. Balwhidder, our narrator, who reveals himself in this passage. So anxious is Mr. Balwhidder that we not think for one moment he is claiming for himself an honor he does not possess that he *seems* willing to interrupt a dying man who can speak only "with difficulty." This is egotistical humility in action.

The suspended quotation, then, is neither a device invented by the Victorians to fill a need nor one whose miscellaneous possibilities they were the first to discover. And this, to put things rather negatively, is what particularly interests me here. If we go back to the biological comparisons of chapter 1, we may say that the suspended quotation is a species whose population increases wildly in certain stretches of English fiction during the fourth, fifth, and sixth decades of the nineteenth century, and that in the terrain we call serious fiction, it grew nowhere as luxuriantly as in the novels of Charles Dickens. What are we to make of this temporary upsurge in population?

I gave some figures in the preceding chapter which suggest the popularity of suspensions in the first half of the nineteenth century, and in the next chapter I'll ask you to consider some more statistics. Right now, though, what we must do is get the rhythm of suspended quotations in our ears. Here, then, is an example from *Jorrocks' Jaunts and Jollities:*

"Pray Mister J——," said she, taking no more notice of the Yorkshireman than if he had been enveloped in Jack the Giant-Killer's coat of darkness, "what is the meaning of this card? I found it in your best coat pocket, which you had on last night and I do desire, sir, that you will tell me how it came there. Good morning sir (spying the Yorkshireman at last), perhaps you know where Mr. Jorrocks was last

> night, and perhaps you can tell me who this person is whose card I have found in the corner of Mr. Jorricks' best coat pocket?"
>
> [chap. 4, p. 59]

Even earlier, in 1818, suspensions had appeared three times on one page of Scott's *The Heart of Midlothian* (chap. 29, p. 310). For example:

> "Eh, Frank Levitt," said this new-comer, who entered with a hop, step, and jump, which at once conveyed her from the door into the center of the party, "were ye killing our mother? or were ye cutting the grunter's weasand that Tam brought in this morning?"

In *Sybil* (1845), so deeply a hungry forties book, we find Disraeli writing

> "Liza Gray," said a woman with black beady eyes, and a red nose, speaking in a sharp voice, and rushing up to a pretty slatternly woman in a straw bonnet, with a dirty babe at her breast: "you know the person I'm looking for."
>
> [III, chap. 3, p. 159]

> "So you see, my father," said Sybil with animation, and dropping her book, which, however, her hand did not relinquish, "even then all was not lost. The stout earl retired beyond the Trent, and years and reigns elapsed before this part of the island accepted their laws and customs."
>
> [III, chap. 5, p. 171]

And in Thackeray's *The Virginians* (1859) the thing flourishes:

> "Our hostess," said my Lord Chesterfield, to his friend in a confidential whisper, of which the utterer did not in the least know the loudness, "puts me in mind of Covent Garden in my youth."
>
> [chap. 27, p. 289]

I compared the sudden upsurge in the popularity of the suspended quotation to a sudden growth in the distribution of a certain plant. But of course when this happens with a plant or animal, the question one asks first is, what ecological opening, what abundance of food, lack of competing species and lack of predators made this growth possible? When this happens with a stylistic device, the question (for those who *will* ask a question) is more likely to be teleological: what end did this device serve, what thing could it accomplish which the novelists of this period wanted to accomplish again and again—and which Dickens, presumably, was especially eager to accomplish?

I have found that when I put this question to experienced readers of Dickens, the answer almost always has something to do with Dickens's sense of the dramatic, his sense that speech is not merely a string of words but words accompanied by gesture, tone, expression. It was, I believe, Earle Davis who first brought to the modern reader's attention Mamie Dickens's wonderful description of her father at work:

> He suddenly jumped from his chair and rushed to a mirror which hung near, and in which I could see the reflection of some extraordinary facial contortions which he was making. He returned rapidly to his desk, wrote furiously for a few moments, and then went again to the mirror. The facial pantomime was resumed, and then . . . he began talking rapidly in a low voice. Ceasing this soon, however, he returned once more to his desk, where he remained silent writing until luncheon time.[3]

Almost certainly those trips to the mirror were for purposes of research, and the results of that research almost certainly appear in many Dickensian suspensions. And is this not our explanation: surely the suspension is so often there in Dickens because the suspension is such a handy place to put information, gestures, facial contortions, and so forth. Borrowing a term from the linguists, we may call this line of explanation the argument from suprasegmentals: "suprasegmentals" being (for our purposes) all the things a speaker does with tone, stress, pitch, loudness, gesture, expression, etc. which add to the meaning of his speech and cannot be indicated by merely writing out the words he utters.

There is much to be said for this line of explanation. Suprasegmentals are going to cause special difficulties for anyone writing lifelike dialogue. Suprasegmentals are the things which most conspicuously separate spoken from written English. (It is in large part because a conversationalist normally does use various suprasegmentals that many people who make themselves understood very well *viva voce* may express themselves poorly, ambiguously, in writing: one writes clearly when one has learned to compensate for the lack of suprasegmentals.) Thus, if one wants to create the impression of real speech, such language as men do use in the way men do use it, surely one ought first of all to find some way to present suprasegmentals. And how should one do this? The problem after all is that the written language is single track, a linear sequence, *segmental*, and by definition suprasegmentals exist simultaneously with rather than as items in a linear sequence. What more appropriate and expressive container for information about suprasegmentals than the suspension, which, though of course it needs must be linear in fact, seems as it were linear only under duress, seems to wish it could just be squeezed in and balanced over a caret.

Yes, this line of argument looks plausible enough. Dickens himself might well have agreed with it. And yet I don't: I certainly grant that a large number of Victorian suspensions are concerned either initially or entirely with suprasegmentals; I agree that the placement of suprasegmentals in suspensions is expressive, dynamic; I believe the very plausibility of the argument from suprasegmentals is a fact of considerable importance. But I don't think the Victorian epidemic of suspensions is fundamentally caused by a deep interest in the way men and women speak.

It's now my job to point out weak spots in the analysis just presented, propose a superior one, and make some sense out of a situation where the weaker analysis is the one most intelligent readers of Victorian fiction would likely endorse, and which, I believe, Dickens and a number of other Victorian novelists would themselves have endorsed. The last of these three things is the easiest to do. Suprasegmentals *are* connected with the fashion for suspended quotations; but the interest in suprasegmentals is excuse rather than cause. The concern with suprasegmentals is a cover, hiding the device's real purpose from both the reader *and the writer himself.* Or, better, let me say that the concern with suprasegmentals *half* conceals the writer's true purpose. The true explanation is a mildly embarrassing one.

As for the weak or questionable spots in the argument from suprasegmentals: notice, to begin with, that at least a largish minority of Victorian suspensions are *not* concerned with suprasegmentals. Then consider the odd place of Surtees on my list: suspensions seem to occur more frequently in *Handley Cross* than in any of the "serious" forties novels I have examined. This ought to make us a bit suspicious: Surtees is interested in the way people speak, but he is interested in the way people speak only when they speak in an amusing or grotesque way. The significance of Surtees's taste for suspended quotations is as it were underscored by Elizabeth Gaskell's reticence in using them. Gaskell certainly knows that the device exists (she does occasionally employ it; she has read novels in which it is used heavily) and Gaskell is deeply interested in the way people actually speak: surely, if the suspended quotation is understood to be primarily a handy way to indicate tone of voice and accompanying gestures, one might expect to find it used heavily in *Mary Barton?* More important, consider for a moment a fact which will concern us a good deal in the next chapter: the "mature" Dickens, the Dickens of the sixties, does not strew his text as freely with suspended quotations as the Dickens of the forties. Why? Surely the later Dickens is not less interested in tone and gesture than the earlier one? And then, too, consider all the naturalistic novelists who take (and give) pains recording dialectal speech in the post-Dickensian period. How many of them use suspensions with a *Barnaby Rudge* exuberance? Why don't they? Are they not interested in the way women and men really speak? Don't they know about the importance of suprasegmentals? Surely they haven't found a device more efficient than the suspension for indicating tone and gesture?

Of course not one of these questions and objections is absolutely crushing, but taken as a group they do diminish the commonsense attractiveness of the original explanation. One might be able to improve the argument from suprasegmentals, but it would seem prudent to look for an alternative explanation before patching up this one.

Now in looking for that alternative explanation, let us also take an alternative approach: the suprasegmental theory is the one which first occurs and appeals to readers when they begin by considering the content of Dickensian suspensions. Logically, there is no reason not to continue with the analysis of content and look for a different common denominator in the statements made in suspensions: certainly we will want to do so at some point in this investigation. Psychologically, though, we may find it more invigorating to come at the problem from a new direction and consider form rather than content. And here a second procedure may prove stimulating: when trying to make sense of an uncommon pattern of usage, we may begin with those examples of the pattern which are the strangest of the strange and hope those oddest cases and most bizarre subvarieties will suggest something about less startling examples.

The extreme case, most bizarre form, of the suspended quotation is what may be called the catchword suspended quotation: a suspended quotation in which a word or phrase quoted just before the authorial interruption is repeated after it. And, to make our view odder still, let us move away from the Victorians themselves and take as our first examples of the device some highly flavored twentieth-century specimens. Breathe this hothouse air before reconsidering *Oliver Twist:*

> "Then who, pray," demanded his interrogator, for, being the wife of a Cape magistrate, she considered herself responsible for the morals of all who met her, and not responsible for those of the lost legion who did not, "who, pray, is that lady in the sunbonnet over there, who, I am told,

shares your stateroom, sir, where, for some reason, she always takes her meals?"

[John Collier, *His Monkey Wife*, 1931, chap. 4, pp. 60–61]

"Now you know what 'hot chocolate' has come to in Switzerland. My mother," she continued, turning to Julia (who, with the revelatory *sans-gêne* of the Past Tense, though actually she prided herself on her reticence, had lunged with her little spoon toward Hugh's cup and collected a sample), "my mother actually broke into tears when she was first served this stuff, because she remembered so tenderly the chocolate of her chocolate childhood."

[Vladimir Nabokov, *Transparent Things*, chap. 13, p. 47]

When I was nineteen years old Sickert told me how to paint a picture. "Mon petit," he said (or at least he said something of the kind, for this, it must be remembered, took place about half a century ago) "mon petit, it's dead easy, there's nothing to it."

[Quentin Bell, "The Artist in Character," *TLS*, May 14, 1976][4]

Now, still moving circuitously toward the hungry forties, we shall, to make the strangeness of this technique of quoting appear odder still, to sensitize ourselves further, contrast what we have just seen with another form and context of quotation: the norms of the King James Bible.

Needless to say, the Victorians knew the rhythms and norms of the Authorized Version very well indeed, far better than we are likely to know them. But all of us know those norms well enough for this particular exercise in gospel idiom. Here, following hard upon Armande's mother's chocolate childhood, are four versions of a verse (not outstandingly familiar) from Luke 9. None of the versions is entirely accurate, but notice that you have a strong sense of the *degree* of wrongness in the different versions, and that the different versions affect you in different ways:

1. Herod said, "John have I beheaded: but who is this, of whom I hear such things?"
2. "John have I beheaded: but who is this of whom I hear such things?" said Herod.
3. "John have I beheaded," said Herod. "But who is this of whom I hear such things?"
4. "John have I beheaded," said Herod. "John have I beheaded: but who is this of whom I hear such things?"

What follows is, I hope, a fair description of your reactions. The first rewriting sounds properly biblical—and, except for the omission of an initial *and*, it is indeed the King James text. Version 2 has a neutral, unmeaning oddness. It probably does seem inauthentic because it fails to give us the tag-before-quotation sequence which is almost always found in the Bible. But, except insofar as we sense that a biblical text ought not to be fooled with, we cannot say that the version 2 arrangement is expressive in any way. Version 3, which employs the inquit, is slightly odder than version 2. The difference clearly does not arise because one form of quotation is found in the Bible and the other is not; what we sense is not authenticity versus inauthenticity but rather that the inauthentic final tag of the second version belongs with the authentic initial tag as a noninterruptive form; the inquit *does* interrupt, and though the inquit has been with us since at least Plato's time we can still sense that there is something fancy about it in comparison to external forms of tagging: the speaker's words are not reverently conveyed as an unbroken whole but in an artful intertwining of description and quotation (or, as we are more likely to put the thing to ourselves, the third version sounds like a novel and the second doesn't). Version 3, then, is *slightly* odder than version 2; but see what happens when we model versions of a more familiar verse upon 2 and 3:

5. "Let there be light," said God.
6. "Let there," said God, "be light."

Here the inquit wholly transforms the verse, which becomes not somewhat odd but grotesque. The inquit—intrusive, officious, bathetic—changes everything; the final tag does not. (This particular inquit, we should notice, is especially intrusive because it occurs at a point in the quoted sentence where the speaker of that sentence—be he human or divine—is unlikely to pause. Most novelistic inquits are in fact placed so that they begin at a point where the speaker *is* likely to pause; but a good novelist knows how to use a countersyntactical inquit for special effects.)[5]

Now heighten the effect even further. In looking at versions 1 through 4, all readers must feel that with version 4 and the introduction of the catchword technique comes an enormous increase in oddity: no one can take version 4 seriously. It need hardly be added that a catchword Genesis is still more preposterous:

7. "Let there," said God, "let there be light."

Inauthenticity has become blasphemy: version 7 presents a God who is not only interruptible but waits upon the convenience of writer and reader. If by chance we were not quite ready to listen to him the first time, or were not listening carefully enough, this God can be made to start over again. He is compliant; possibly he has a nervous stutter. In any case, version 7 is no way to create a world. One feels all of this when the catchword suspension is used with inappropriate material—or more exactly, when even a simple catchword quotation is used with the wrong material: for notice that our offending wedge has never been anything more than an inoffensive two syllables. Obviously the catchword quotation is not just another option. There are places (or, as we now know, there is at least one very important place) where it simply cannot be employed. It is easy enough to devise a rule here: the catchword quotation is not suitable for use with speakers too prominent, dignified, important, to be interrupted, and Judaeo-Christian reality includes at least one such character. The important thing here is of course the sense of *an* interruption. If the catchword quotation interrupts the one who is quoted, so, obviously, does the catchword suspended quotation, and so (a bit less obviously) does any suspended quotation. And *habitual* interruption, in art as in life, is aggression.

The next part seems obvious enough: from aggression to jealousy in a few paragraphs. But I am not certain that here the most direct movement is the best one. Truly to understand the Dickensian suspended quotation is to have a strong sense of its complex and overdetermined life; not enough to see what the thing is at bottom: one should feel the distance between bottom and surface, must not think those waters between bottom and surface less turbid than they are, must never forget how brilliantly and variously light plays on the surface of these waters. There is a fundamental meaning to the Dickensian suspended quotation, and both author and reader perceive that meaning. But both perceive it intermittently, distractedly. The device has surface uses, middle level significance. It will be better not to get right to the bottom of things but to look around a little.

We shall stay with the catchword suspension for a while but turn from the places where it is not to be found to those where it is. The age of Dickens, again, is its favorite habitat; there the twentieth-century exotic flourishes like a weed:

> "And so, Amy," said her sister, when the three together passed out, at the door that had such a shame-faced consciousness of being different from other doors: the uncle instinctively taking Amy's arm as the arm to be relied on: "so, Amy, you are curious about me?"
>
> [*LD*, I, chap. 19, p. 223]

But just as the grotesque unsuitability of this form in a sacred text is a fact to bear in mind in trying to understand the area in which it does flourish, so too the Darkbloomish afterlife of the device, its occasional appearance in very stylized twentieth-century prose is a thing to recall while considering the Victorian age. For it seems possible that when Dickens started to use the device, it already suggested something very mannered, had strong associations (as, of course, Dickens himself did in his first prosperity) with Regency dandyism.

"Seems possible" is perhaps the most that can be said. As

usual, there is no direct evidence (no helpful comments by Dickens himself), and it seems quite clear that Dickens would have encountered catchword suspensions in works (for example, *Castle Rackrent, The Heart of Midlothian*)[6] having nothing of the precious about them. The possibility I am talking about here is suggested not by historical evidence but by esthetic judgment: the catchword suspension is especially noticeable in dandiacal writing because it seems so much at home, so expressive there. And what it expresses in Regency narration is a set of relations among author, narrator, characters, and readers which is complexly like and unlike the relationships we will find in, for example, that *Great Expectations* forge scene. Let us spend a few moments looking at those similarities and dissimilarities.

I will start with a rather Nabokovian passage from Keats's *The Cap and Bells.* The character Keats describes and then quotes in this part of his Regency narrative is the prince—and the prince is almost certainly a caricature of the prince regent himself:

> He rose, he stampt his foot, he rang the bell,
> And ordered some death-warrants to be sent
> For signature:- somewhere the tempest fell,
> As many a poor felon does not live to tell.
>
> XXI
>
> "At the same time Eban,"—(this was his page
> A fay of colour, slave from top to toe,
> Sent as a present, while yet under age,
> From the Viceroy of Zanguebar,—wise, slow
> His speech, his only words were "yes" and "no,"
> But swift of look, and foot, and wing was he,)—
> "At the same time, Eban, this instant go
> To Hum the soothsayer, whose name I see
> Among the fresh arrivals in our empery . . ."

The tyrannical prince, waited on by slaves, is given poetical punishment even as he issues his commands. When we introduced the catchwords quotation into Genesis we produced blasphemy; here Keats suggests *lèse-majesté:* he interrupts the prince as the latter issues orders, and he does this so that we may be told about—a slave! Worse still, it does rather look as though Keats has interrupted the prince and then, with the recurrence of the catchword, made him begin his sentence over again ("At the same time, Eban . . . At the same time, Eban")—this, presumably, for the reader's convenience. Now the similarity between the antityrannical use of the catchword suspension here and the antityrannical function of the plain suspension in the Mrs. Joe passage is clear enough. What I do want to emphasize is the difference. Tyrants both the prince and Mrs. Joe are, but they tyrannize in different social areas, stand in quite different relations to the quoters of their words, and, perhaps most important, tyrannize in utterly different styles. The pseudo-Pip who narrates *Great Expectations* is Mrs. Joe's social superior—clearly we do not have a comparable relationship in *The Cap and Bells:* Regency literature is a literature of high life. Second, in our Mrs. Joe paragraph the authorial chattiness disrupts a speech of great (even if artificially induced) emotional energy; in the age and literature of dandyism, authorial chattiness and pseudocarelessness about the right ordering and presentation of material does not contrast with but echoes the attitudes of the characters themselves, who either are or strive to appear as lacking in diligence as they can possibly be: it is this echoic function which gives the device its particular force, its esthetic rightness, in dandiacal works. Dickens's Mrs. Joe is constantly doing things; she works, as we say, like a demon; the faery prince Keats interrupts has been lying on a sofa in his cabinet [ll. 133–34], and we'll soon learn that, when he has issued his orders to Eban,

> the Prince, in half a pet,
> Let o'er the silk his propping elbow slide,
> Caught up his little legs, and in a fret,
> Fell on the sofa on his royal side.
> The slave retreated backwards, humble-eyed . . .
>
> [ll. 199–203]

(In fact, Keats's prince is a somewhat atypical Regency hero not so much because he is nonhuman as because he can allow it to be seen that he is "in half a pet.") Usually, the Regency catchword quotation is the author behaving like a Regency hero who has his cup of chocolate brought in at two in the afternoon, decides it is still a bit too early to rise, and then has a fresh cup brought in at four. A Regency hero is never in a hurry, or ought never to seem in a hurry; his life is devoted to *not* getting on with the things which are central to the lives of inferior beings. The dandy makes the peripheral and prefatory (for example, dressing oneself) into the central. The author using a catchword suspension—or, indeed, *any* longish suspension—may be said to be doing the same thing: the speech, the thing of central importance, is stopped so that ancillary details may be given, accompanying circumstances indicated. Here also the peripheral becomes central. The Regency catchword suspension parodies, imitates, almost emblemizes the dandiacal life, in which being is more important than doing or becoming and in which linear movement, getting on, is a thing for the vulgar. Thus the first speech in Disraeli's *Vivian Grey* begins:

> "I am told, my dear," observed Mrs. Grey, one day after dinner to her husband, "I am told, my dear, that Dr. Flummery's would do very well for Vivian. . . ."
>
> [1, p. 1]

We find in Bulwer's *Pelham*, the central work of dandyism, such passages as:

> "Let me," I said, when I found myself alone with my second, "let me thank you most cordially for your assistance; and allow me to cultivate an acquaintance so singularly begun. . . ."
>
> [I, chap. 13, p. 40]
>
> "Hem!" said Mr. Aberton, thrusting his large hand through his lank light hair. "Hem—could one do anything, do you think, in that quarter?"
>
> [I, chap. 18, p. 65][7]

And in Frederick Marryat's "How to Write a Fashionable

Novel" (1833), a satire upon books like *Pelham*, it is suggested that the late-rising hero of a dandiacal work might be presented as rebuking his servant thus:

> "'Coridon,' said he, surveying his attendant from head to foot, and ultimately assuming a severity of countenance, 'Coridon, you are becoming gross, if not positively what the people call *fat*'. . . ."
>
> [p. 65]

When Disraeli transforms himself from a Regency into a hungry forties novelist he will now and again use catchword suspensions for Dickensian lower-class characters. But it seems clear that Disraeli uses the device more lavishly, comfortably, and lovingly when he is presenting the other of his two nations—quoting those characters who would have been eligible inhabitants of earlier, dandiacal fictions:

> "I understand, then," said Lord Marney to his brother, as on the evening of the same day they were seated together in the drawing-room, in close converse—"I understand, then, that you have in fact paid nothing, and that my mother will give you a thousand pounds. That won't go very far."
>
> [II, chap. 6, p. 68]

And little more than one page later we find:

> "You were speaking of the election, George," said Egremont, not without reluctance, yet anxious, as the ice had been broken, to bring the matter to a result. Lord Marney, before the election, had written, in reply to his mother consulting him on the step, a letter with which she was delighted, but which Egremont at the time could have wished to have been more explicit. However, in the excitement attendant on a first contest, and influenced by the person whose judgment always swayed, and, in the present case, was peculiarly entitled to sway him, he stifled his scruples, and persuaded himself that he was a candidate not only with the sanction but at the insistence of his brother. "You were speaking of the election, George," said Egremont.

Egremont is a Regency aristocrat becoming a Victorian hero; salvation is making oneself a life which is not a catchword suspension writ large.

Now by the time Disraeli publishes *Sybil*, Dickens has already created a large number of truly Dickensian catchword suspensions, has already made the frequent occurrence of such quotations part of the rhythm of Dickensian narration, narration of life far from the beau monde:

> "In one word, sir," said Mr. Pickwick, "is my servant right in suspecting that a certain Captain Fitz-Marshall is in the habit of visiting here? Because," added Mr. Pickwick, as he saw Mr. Nupkins was about to offer a very indignant interruption, "because if he be, I know that person to be a ——"
>
> [*PP*, chap. 25, p. 345]

> "Have you," said Mr. Tappertit, letting his gaze fall on the party indicated, who was indeed the new knight, by this time restored to his own apparel: "Have you the impression of your street-door key in wax?"
>
> [*BR*, chap. 8, p. 67]

> "And do you suppose, sir," retorted Mr. Tappertit, with a thickness and slowness of speech which contrasted forcibly with the rapidity and earnestness of his kind-hearted master—"and do you suppose, sir, that I am base and mean enough to accept your servile proposition? Miscreant!"
>
> [*BR*, chap. 51, p. 391]

The question is, what does the essentially disruptive and contrastive Dickensian suspension owe to the essentially paradistic and emblematic Regency suspension? The answer here is, the social cachet which belonged to the *author* of Regency works. The Regency suspension is a device used *by* an urbane writer, and I suspect Charles Dickens relished the associations with urbanity and knowledge of the beau monde the device had; relished these even when his target of choice was a character like Ralph Nickleby—or, indeed, Mrs. Joe.

Here we move inevitably to biography. Charles Dickens was a man with strong dandiacal tendencies, and we may recall that a proper Regency novel had to be (or at least be thought) a *roman à clef*, its author a member of the world he describes.[8] Dickens quite likes a moderately foppish style, even when he is not writing about fops; he likes to seem—no, not a chilly aristocrat, certainly, but a bit of a swell. Again: the catchword quotation is very much a device for gentlemen who write with ease. Such quotations suggest *negligent* composition, even a studied carelessness; it is as though the author were saying, "I began that quotation before I was *quite* ready for it—but, oh well, let it stand; I'll explain what I must, and then start over again." It is suggestive to look at the suspended quotation as a deliberately careless device, because in the first part of his career Dickens rather fancies elegantly *négligé* prose. His casualness is displayed in the correction-of-ambiguous-pronoun tic, which one encounters both in the early novels and in Dickens's personal letters. For example:

> What was the learned man's astonishment, when that unaccountable person flung the money on the pavement, and requested in figurative terms to be allowed the pleasure of fighting him (Mr. Pickwick) for the amount!
>
> [*PP*, chap. 1, p. 7]

It need hardly be pointed out that the negligence here is simply for effect: clearly Dickens could have deleted the *him*, removed the parenthesis around *Mr. Pickwick*, and had an unexceptionable sentence. The air of insouciance is deliberately cultivated: "Oh well, let it stand."[9] "Him (Mr. Pickwick)": a schoolmaster—Bradley Headstone, for instance—would not, could not, permit himself this slovenliness; but one is rather more like Wrayburn than like Headstone; one is rather like milor Byron:

> XC
>
> Young Juan wandered by the glassy brooks,
> Thinking unutterable things; he threw
> Himself at length within the leafy nooks
> Where the wild branch of the cork forest grew;
> There poets find materials for their books,

And every now and then we read them through,
So that their plan and prosody are eligible,
Unless, like Wordsworth, they prove unintelligible.

XCI

He, Juan (and not Wordsworth), so pursued
His self-communion with his own high soul. . . .[10]

The connection between this studied insouciance in the use of pronouns and the Dickensian catchword quotation (here indirect) is perhaps nowhere more clearly seen than on the second page of *Pickwick Papers:*

> A casual observer, adds the secretary, to whose notes we are indebted for the following account—a casual observer might possibly have remarked nothing extraordinary in the bald head, and circular spectacles, which were intently turned toward his (the secretary's) face, during the reading of the above resolutions.

It is hardly a new discovery that Dickens is an extremely complex figure: the champion of the poor and oppressed does go in for curls and embroidered waistcoats; the young writer deeply anxious about sales, believing in hard work, respectful of and wanting to win a popular audience, cultivates mannerisms of a dandiacal *laissez-aller* style. Such a device as the catchword suspension will serve a number of Dickens's needs both professional and personal. Its Regency association will give him, as author, an unfair, snobbish, quite reprehensible superiority over most of the characters he injures in the very act of interruption; will give him, in fact, a sort of advantage Charles Dickens would be most unwilling to think carefully about. That same Regency association does suit him personally, especially in the years of curls and fancy waistcoats: the Regency style is the style of authors who are of the beau monde. The association is somewhere in the background of the older Pip's urbanity as he interrupts Mrs. Joe.

Through the years when Regency literature was being written, or was at least fresh in the memory, the catchword suspension probably had a special social cachet, and one wants to be aware of this in considering what it means for Dickens to take up the habit of frequently interrupting. But more interesting than the social overtones a particular device just happened to have at a particular time and place are questions about the overtones, suggestions, nuances, even problems a verbal device produces through its place within a linguistic system. Here, then, we may take up an odd sort of ambiguity the catchword suspension brings to the system of quotation characteristic of the nineteenth-century English novel. When presenting pseudobiblical catchword quotations—"Let there," said God, "let there be light"—I spoke about the creation of a stuttering God, a God who starts his speeches over again. Now I want to consider that stutter a bit more nicely. How ought one to interpret the catchword? The reader can hardly ever be certain; the Victorian catchword quotation is almost always ambiguous: readers of Dickens see the form on page after page but cannot, in most cases, be sure what Dickens is indicating about the utterance being recorded. What would an unedited transcript of our last speech from *Barnaby Rudge* be? Did Sim Tappertit utter the words "and do you suppose, sir" once or twice? An experienced reader of Victorian writings will know precedents for both interpretations. There are some passages in nineteenth-century literature where the catchword repetition clearly *is* editorial; where the writer, in other words, feels free to quote twice the words his character is supposed to have used only once.[11] On the other hand, period style makes phrasal repetition by the character seem more plausible in the nineteenth-century than it is now, or, I believe, than it was in the eighteenth century. Thus, for instance, in Scott's *Waverley* we read:

> "And why will not you, Miss Mac-Ivor, who can so well describe a happy union, why will not you be yourself the person you describe?"
>
> [chap. 27, p. 375]

Rhythmically, this is quite easy to transform into a catchword suspended quotation—for example,

> "And why will not you," said he, raising his eyes from the album into which her verses had been copied, "why will not you be yourself the person you describe?"

Inquit might be substituted for vocative in such Trollopean speeches as:

> "I do think, Lady Fawn, I do think that is the greatest shame I ever heard."
>
> [*Eustace Diamonds*, chap. 33, p. 398]

> "But there are occasions, Miss Vavasour; there are occasions when the ordinary laws by which we govern our social conduct must be made somewhat elastic."
>
> [*Can You Forgive Her?*, chap. 26, p. 251] [12]

Now the ambiguity of the Victorian catchword suspension is a curious fact and may be thought of as having two different functions. First, the catchword suspension is implicitly subversive of the value system implicit in the new convention, strict constructionist nineteenth-century novel. In Victorian fiction, as I suggested in the previous chapter, a character's speech is privileged discourse. It is set off by quotation marks, and by quotation marks which separate the quoted words from the inquit far more fastidiously than does punctuation in either the earlier English or the contemporary French novel. A change of speakers normally brings a shift of paragraph: not only is the exchange of remarks an event worth marking with a new paragraph, but each part of that exchange is a major event. Often we will have *erlebte Rede* and recognize characterly mannerisms within an authorial summary, rather than transcription of the character's speech or thoughts. But *erlebte Rede* is a bonus, an extracontractual award to the audience: the reader is given greater proximity to the character's very words than the formal qualities of indirect discourse had promised. (*Erlebte Rede* is the equivalent of a musical encore: more of a good thing; something extra. This is one reason why *erlebte Rede* functions so well as a comic device: local satiric use can be combined with the formal exuberance of overmeasure.) In the nineteenth-century strict constructionist novel there is no converse to *erlebte Rede:* such a converse, an overflowing of narration into direct quotation, would be adulteration, whereas *erlebte Rede* is enrichment. Of the frequently encountered devices of Dickensian fiction, only the ambiguous catchword quotation subverts the system of privilege and suggests that quotation marks are not an absolutely trustworthy guarantee of the speech's integrity. And it is just here that the *ambiguity* of the device is essential. If one knew just how the catchword quotation ought to be read in a particular case, then the device would complicate the reportorial system of these novels but not subvert it. As matters stand, the ambiguity of the catchword suspension is the one sign that the author does not regard direct quotation as a sacred trust—that he is careless, sloppy, unreverential, after he has signalled his intent to give us a character's very words.

Second, if we take it as axiomatic that the more one distorts a character's *ipsissima verba* the more one injures that character, then the ambiguity of the catchword suspension keeps us from seeing just how much damage has been done: in this respect the formal ambiguity of the device corresponds to the ambiguity of intent (or deceptiveness of intent) we discover in "kindly," "helpful" suspensions of speeches made by sympathetic characters.

Now here at last, with that second function of the catchword suspension's ambiguity, I do come back to my central hypothesis: the radical aggressiveness not simply of catchword suspensions but of all suspended quotations. What will such a hypothesis do? What will it explain?

We start with some things already observed. Insofar as one thinks of the repetition in a catchword quotation as editorial rather than original, one senses a sort of *lèse-majesté*, a rudeness toward the character: that character becomes the butt of a Bergsonian joke. He starts to speak but then his talk is stopped by a power over which he has no control (and of which he has no knowledge) and then started over again by that same power. Any sort of suspension is basically interference, and people (including authors) who make a habit of interfering and interrupting are being aggressive, hostile. Both Dickens and his audience knew it was not polite to interrupt and neither Dickens nor his audience separated life from literature with the niceness of a modern academic. Both author and audience would have sensed a sort of rudeness in the frequent suspensions characteristic of *The Old Curiosity Shop* and *Barnaby Rudge.* Dickens's audience would have felt (though not mentioned) that underlying aggressiveness, and what they felt helped give their experience of Dickensian fiction its particular quality.

In narration or at cocktail party, habitual interruption is aggressive. But let us circle back to what it is that Dickens says when he interrupts his characters. An analysis of the content of those Dickensian suspensions will certainly help make a case for the aggressiveness reading quite as well as it helps make a case for the suprasegmentals theory. My argument here is simply based upon quantity: the Dickensian suspension is overtly, locally aggressive a great deal of the time. Thus, of course, the passage from *Great Expectations* discussed at the beginning of this chapter; thus the quotations from Sim Tappertit a few pages back: time after time we find suspensions in which what is said is distinctly unflattering to the character whose speech is being interrupted. Dickens does of course talk about suprasegmentals in many of these suspensions—but how uncomplimentary that talk tends to be!

> "I am proud to see," said Mr. Carker, with a servile stooping of his neck, which the revelations making by his eyes and teeth proclaim to be a lie, "I am proud to see that my humble offering is graced by Mrs. Dombey's hand. . . ."
>
> [*DS*, chap. 31, p. 444]

> "And how," asked Mr. Pecksniff, drawing off his gloves and warming his hands before the fire, as benevolently as if they were someone else's, not his: "and how is he now?"
>
> [*MC*, chap. 3, p. 33]

The *fleurs du mal* are nipped in the bud, not even born when blasted.

We have, in the following passage from the *Pickwick* trial scene, a revealing use of the punitive suspension. The passage is certainly amusing but not *quite* as amusing as it might have been. Here Sam Weller is being questioned by Serjeant Buzfuz:

> "Do you mean to tell me, Mr. Weller," said Serjeant Buzfuz, folding his arms emphatically and turning half-round to the jury, as if in mute assurance that he would bother the witness yet: "Do you mean to tell me, Mr. Weller, that you saw nothing of this fainting on the part of the plaintiff in the arms of the defendant, which you heard described by the witnesses?"
>
> "Certainly not," replied Sam. "I was in the passage 'till they called me up, and then the old lady was not there."
>
> "Now, attend, Mr. Weller," said Serjeant Buzfuz, dipping a large pen into the inkstand before him, for the purpose of frightening Sam with a show of taking down his answer. "You were in the passage, and yet saw nothing of what was going forward. Have you a pair of eyes, Mr. Weller?"
>
> "Yes, I have a pair of eyes," replied Sam, "and that's just it. If they wos a pair o' patent double million magnifyin' gas microscopes of hextra power, p'raps I might be able to see through a flight o' stairs and a deal door; but bein' only eyes, you see, my wision's limited."
>
> At this answer, which was delivered without the slightest appearance of irritation, and with the most complete simplicity and equanimity of manner, the spectators tittered, the little judge smiled, and Serjeant Buzfuz looked particularly foolish.
>
> [chap. 34, pp. 484–85]

Dickens does not always use a suspension when quoting Serjeant Buzfuz in this interrogation of Sam, but he clearly wants those suspensions which are used to be meted out to the pompous, rhetorically aggressive serjeant rather than to the admirable Weller. And just because he wishes to assign suspensions to the talk of the unsympathetic and not the sympathetic character, Dickens makes Sam's comic answer less comic than it might be. The problem with Weller's second reply, as we have it in the fourth paragraph, is that as we read those words, we likely *do* assume there is a certain sarcasm or irritability in Sam's voice; and thus we miss half the fun. Allow me to make Dickens funnier by rearranging the words in those two last paragraphs:

> "Yes," replied Sam, without the slightest appearance of irritation, and with the most complete simplicity and equanimity of manner, "I have a pair of eyes, and that's just it. If they wos a pair o' patent double million magnifyin' gas microscopes of hextra power, p'rhaps I might be able to see through a flight o' stairs and a deal door; but bein' only eyes, you see, my wision's limited."
>
> The spectators tittered, the little judge smiled, and Serjeant Buzfuz looked particularly foolish.

This splendid improvement did not occur to Dickens (or at least was not made by Dickens) because he wanted to reserve suspended quotations here for the serjeant and not intrude himself into the speeches of the good cockney.

Again, it is indicative of the strong association of suspended quotation and counteraggression, the punishment of evil and stripping away of disguises, that in *Dombey and Son* Dickens uses the device more than three times as often when Major Joe Bagstock presents Dombey to Edith and Mrs. Skewton as he does when moving toward the death of Little Paul.[13]

As we read through Dickens, then, we will find, in almost any fifty pages, several examples of knavery exposed and punished in and by suspended quotations. But, in considering the hostility of the device, one ought to consider, along with these justly punitive suspensions, another very large group—suspensions for comic effect. For comedy, after all, the comedy of having fun at someone's expense, is a form of aggression.[14] Thus, in *Dombey and Son* one finds not only a good number of interruptions of Carker, Mrs. Skewton, and Major Bagstock, but such charming passages as:

> "Bunsby!" said Captain Cuttle, who would seem to have estimated the value of his distinguished friend's opinions in

> proportion to the immensity of the difficulty he experienced in making anything out of them; "Bunsby," said the Captain, quite confounded by admiration, "you carry a weight of mind easy, as would swamp one of my tonnage soon. . . ."
>
> [chap. 39, p. 553]

In *Pickwick Papers*, even though there are indeed characters like Serjeant Buzfuz who deserve and receive punishment, comic suspensions are the most striking ones, the targets of choice speakers at moments of innocent self-importance, self-dramatization:

> "My dear friend," said Mr. Ben Allen, taking advantage of Mr. Bob Sawyer's temporary absence behind the counter, whither he had retired to dispense some of the second-hand leeches, previously referred to: "my dear friend, I am very miserable."
>
> [chap. 38, p. 535]

If one counted these things up (and I must confess I would rather assert this than actually go about counting comic suspensions and punitive suspensions), if one did count these things up, one would certainly find that well over half the suspensions (catchword and other) in early Dickens could be described as punitive or comic or (the best of them) both at once: we would certainly find, in other words, that well over half were locally aggressive.

Well over half, however, is not good enough: we have here one of the difficulties I pointed out in discussing the suprasegmentals interpretation: "by their fruits shall ye know them" is a difficult rule to use when there are even a few oranges mixed in with the apples. One does not have to read very far in a Dickens novel to find difficult cases: suspended quotations which are not, in any way recognizable to common sense, locally aggressive. Consider the following, for instance. What reader will believe for a moment that Esther Summerson quotes Allan Woodcourt in a nasty way:

> "Miss Flite," said Mr. Woodcourt, in a grave kind of voice, as if he were appealing to her while speaking to us; and lay-

ing his hand gently on her arm; "Miss Flite describes her illness with her usual accuracy. . . ."

[*BH*, chap. 14, p. 198]

Now that is not an apple but an orange. Esther/Dickens only wishes us to understand, and so admire the more: and to understand and admire the more we need those things tape recorder and film would preserve for us, but verbal transcript cannot. Surely there is no malice here—and surely (as the psychology of interruption might lead us to suspect) there is here no covert self-assertion. From *Esther?* No, no.

Well, I'm going to argue "from Esther, yes, yes" (or at least, "through Esther, yes, yes"): all suspensions are aggressive and self-assertive. First of all, our commonsense, cocktail party understanding of the sort of people who keep interrupting can be shored up with contextual evidence about the way Victorian writers thought about quotation; evidence suggesting that for the Victorians something like the suspended quotation would have seemed radically intrusive.

One thing to consider here is the commonness in nineteenth-century fiction of what I shall call single-channel jokes. Compared with Sterne before and, for example, Nabokov later, Dickens and his contemporaries seem not terribly interested in metafictions; but one Sterne-ish thing they do play with quite often is the relation between the time supposedly taken up by events in the story and the time taken up by the narration of those events. There are places in Victorian fiction where the irrational confounding of these two time schemes has (or seems intended to have) a genuine poignancy. *David Copperfield* is important here, and surely every sympathetic reader of that book responds to the narrator's sense of the past being with him, refusing to stay past. As he comes to that part of the story where Emily runs off with Steerforth, David must keep reminding himself that events narrated *are* over, that they do not happen again in narrational time:

A dread falls on me here. A cloud is lowering on the distant town, towards which I retraced my solitary steps.

> I fear to approach it. I cannot bear to think of what did come, upon that memorable night; of what must come again, if I go on.
>
> It is no worse, because I write of it. It would be no better, if I stopped my most unwilling hand. It is done. Nothing can undo it; nothing can make it other than as it was.
>
> [chap. 31, p. 447]

Far more often, however, that idea of narrational and narrated time being the same, of past events being (re)enacted in present, narrational time, gives rise to little pleasantries, casually tossed off—pleasantries on the model of Sterne's "But I forget my uncle *Toby*, whom all this while we have left knocking the ashes out of his tobacco pipe" [*Tristram Shandy*, I, chap. 21, p. 65]. There is *Jane Eyre*, in which Rochester is at one point looking at Jane's pictures:

> While he is so occupied, I will tell you, reader, what they are: and first, I must promise that they are nothing wonderful. . . .
>
> [chap. 13, p. 147]

Thackeray, as one might expect, will provide us with examples: chapter 8 of *Pendennis* has the heading "In Which Pen is Kept Waiting at The Door While the Reader is Informed Who Little Laura Was"; in *The Newcomes* we have a transitional sentence beginning "All the time we have been making this sketch, Ethel is standing looking at Clive . . ." [I, chap. 24, p. 310]. At one point in Surtees's *Handley Cross*, a new character named Charley Stubbs arrives at Jorrocks' house, and Jorrocks starts rushing to greet him. We then have a ten-page digression in which Surtees tells us about Charley's history and acquaintance with Jorrocks, and then return to the main story line with

> "'Ow are ye, my lad o' wax?" exclaimed Mr. Jorrocks, bouncing out in his sky-blue dressing-gown and slippers, as Charley appeared at the garden gate, where we have most unceremoniously kept him standing during his introduction.
>
> [chap. 19, p. 175]

Trollope, describing the celebration of Frank's coming of age in *Doctor Thorne*, takes the occasion to give his readers some helpful background information and then returns to the foreground of his story by chiding himself: "But we have kept the Greshambury tenantry waiting under the oak-trees by far too long" [chap. 1, p. 12]. Later [chap. 8, p. 90] Trollope apologizes for the tedious way in which he has been describing Frank holding Mary's hand; Trollope's own narrative methods have made it seem the heroine allowed the young man to hold that hand an improperly long time. At the opening of the twenty-seventh chapter of *Oliver Twist*, Dickens plays the same sort of game in a moderately complex, if rather heavy-handed way: the lengthiness of the sentence about keeping a beadle waiting keeps the beadle waiting that much longer:

> As it would be by no means seemly in a humble author to keep so mighty a personage as a beadle waiting, with his back to the fire, and the skirts of his coat gathered up under his arms, until such time as it might suit his pleasure to relieve him, and as it would still less become his station, or his gallantry, to involve in the same neglect a lady on whom that beadle had looked with an eye of tenderness and affection, and in whose ear he had whispered sweet words, which, coming from such a quarter, might well thrill the bosom of maid or matron of whatsoever degree; the historian whose pen traces these words—trusting that he knows his place, and that he entertains a becoming reverence for those upon earth to whom high and important authority is delegated—hastens to pay them that respect which their position demands, and to treat them with all that duteous ceremony which their exalted rank and (by consequence) great virtues, imperatively claim at his hands.

The chapter thus introduced also ends with Bumble under consideration, but then attempts to jolt the reader with another play upon single-channel narrative; suddenly the reader is made to feel a sort of bad Samaritan who has frivolously left Oliver Twist to bleed his life away:

> And now that we have accompanied him [Bumble] so far on his road home, and have made all necessary preparations for the old woman's funeral, let us set on foot a few inquiries after young Oliver Twist, and ascertain whether he be still lying in the ditch where Toby Crackit left him.

Toby Crackit *et tu quoque, lector.*

Now the important point about such single-channel jokes is this. If we can assume, as I believe the wide distribution of these jokes gives us the right to do, that Victorian novelists share the phantasy of narrating time interfering or merging with narrated time, and the storyteller either causing such delays or being on the lookout for ways to avoid causing them, then it would be very odd if the suspended quotation were not felt to be an *interrupted* quotation, an intrusion. Still—Esther Summerson being rude to Allan? We can move in closer. The Victorians are alert to the possibility of an author making characters wait around while he explains something to his readers, share the single-channel phantasy. Significantly, if not surprisingly, this phantasy every now and then produces a joke about dialogue. Two Dickensian examples come to mind. In both of them the author is submissive before a character who seems to have a very firm grip on the one available microphone; both author-subduing characters are garrulous women. *Nicholas Nickleby*'s Miss Knag has been running on for a while, and Dickens says, "Here Miss Knag paused to take breath, and while she pauses it may be observed . . ." [chap. 17, p. 210]. Much the same thing happens with Sarah Gamp in *Martin Chuzzlewit;* Sarah rambles in her usual fashion, and then Dickens writes, "At this point she was fain to stop for breath; and advantage may be taken of this circumstance to state that a fearful mystery surrounded this lady of the name of Harris" [chap. 25, p. 406]. (It will be worth recalling later on that in both these passages—passages where Dickens explicitly connects the single-channel idea and dialogue—the character is thought of as making the author wait rather than the other way around.) In the Victorian novels I know, perhaps the clearest indication that the narrator can be thought of as breaking in upon the speech of a character and forcing that character to wait—that is, in the way Trollope thought of himself as forcing the Greshambury tenantry to wait under the oak trees—comes in Thackeray's *The Newcomes.*

> "How much a glass, think you?" says Fred, filling another bumper. "A half-crown, think ye?—a half-crown, Honeyman? By cock and pye, it is not worth a bender." He says this in the manner of the most celebrated tragedian of the day. He can imitate any actor, tragic or comic; any known Parliamentary orator or clergyman, any saw, cock, cloop of a cork wrenched from a bottle and guggling of wine into the decanter afterwards, bee-buzzing, little boy up a chimney, &c. He imitates people being ill on board a steam-packet so well that he makes you die of laughing: his uncle the Bishop could not resist this comic exhibition, and gave Fred a cheque for a comfortable sum of money; and Fred, getting cash for the cheque at the "Cave of Harmony," imitated his uncle the Bishop and his Chaplain, winding up with his Lordship and the Chaplain being unwell at sea—the Chaplain and the Bishop quite natural and distinct.
>
> "How much does a glass of this sack cost thee, Charley?" *resumes Fred after this parenthesis.* "You say it is not dear. . . ."
>
> [I, chap. 11, pp. 162–63. Italics mine]

Another sort of evidence—indirect but highly interesting—is the way Dickens and his contemporaries render the Pregnant Pause, the significant (ominous or embarrassed or embarrassing or awe-inspired) silence which is ended when some character speaks. Novelistic common sense would seem to dictate simple mimesis for such a moment: first tell what happened first, then what followed, and so grow to a point. And of course sometimes the Victorians do present the pregnant pause in just this way.[15] But they also know a trick worth five of that:[16] instead of the mimetic sequence

1. description of pause

2. quotation of speech ending pause

use the artificial sequence

1. quotation of the opening of the speech
2. inquit, followed by narration of pause
3. quotation of body of speech.

Use this artificial sequence and you can make your reader experience the tension of that pause. The mimetic sequence is inherently like a nail driven into plaster; the artificial one like a nail driven into wood. In this passage from *Hard Times,* for instance, Dickens uses the artificial sequence twice so that we may feel the painfulness of silences in a subdued, almost Trollopian scene:

> "Mrs. Bounderby," said Harthouse, after a short silence, "may there be a better confidence between yourself and me? Tom has borrowed a considerable sum of you."
>
> "You will understand, Mr. Harthouse," she returned, after some indecision: she had been more or less uncertain, and troubled throughout the conversation, and yet had in the main preserved her self-contained manner; "you will understand that if I tell you what you press to know, it is not by way of complaint or regret. . . ."
>
> [II, chap. 7, pp. 171–72]

Elsewhere, Dickens employs this artificial sequence to achieve splendidly grotesque effects:

> "A sulky state of feeling," said Squeers, after a terrible pause, during which he had moistened the palm of his right hand again, "won't do. Cheerfulness and contentment must be kept up. Mobbs, come to me!"
>
> [*NN*, chap. 8, p. 95]

> "What do you think them women does t'other day," continued Mr. Weller, after a short pause, during which he had significantly struck the side of his nose with his fore-finger some half-dozen times. "What do you suppose they does, t'other day, Sammy?"
>
> [*PP*, chap. 22, p. 297]

"It's not Madness, ma'am," replied Mr. Bumble, after a few moments of deep meditation. "It's Meat."

[*OT*, chap. 7, p. 46]

When one looks at *Nicholas Nickleby* or *Dombey and Son*, one finds the artificial sequence used again and again;[17] and, as I have suggested, the device, though a Dickensian favorite, is not idiosyncratically Dickensian:

"What I want to know, George," the old gentleman said, after slowly smacking his first bumper,—"what I want to know is, how you and—ah—that little thing upstairs are carrying on?"

[*Vanity Fair*, I, chap. 13, p. 149]

Interesting in itself, this artificial sequence; one would like to learn its history and fortunes in some detail. But what makes the artificial sequence particularly significant is the fact that the early Victorians understand so well that it *will* make us feel remarkably uncomfortable; will, by indirect means, give us some of the characters' experience of a small, disconcerting gap in time. And in understanding this, what the Victorians understand is that the insertion of an authorial comment into a character's speech is not merely "conventional," value-free: such an insertion is always an interruption of the character, is always experienced by the reader (at least subliminally) as something which causes the character pain—or would cause the character pain if the character knew about it. Because readers of Victorian novels are (generally speaking) nice people, they do not like to witness the inflicting of pain on others: they are uncomfortable at a gathering where one person is interrupted by another, and wait tensely for the interruption to end; are uncomfortable also when an author interrupts a character, and wait for that interruption to end. The artificial sequence is a narrational technique based upon the writer's intuitive understanding of this situation, based upon his exploitation of the reader's discomfort in the presence of interrupted speech.

Single-channel jokes, the artificial sequence, local explications, the cocktail party analogy from real life. One can see that the Victorian suspended quotation often is hostile, and one can see what it is in the nature of the device which allows it to express hostility. But one must then ask, why, if there is something intrinsically nasty about the thing, should such a writer as Dickens ever use the suspended quotation when presenting the speech of characters he genuinely admires and wants us, his readers, to admire?

To answer this question I present a new hypothesis. It seems to me that in many British novels of the eighteen thirties, forties, and fifties, and most intensely in the novels of Charles Dickens, there existed a *literary* class warfare: authors as a class against characters as a class. This is an undeclared war, and it has no ideologists: the combatants go about their work with no clear understanding of why they are doing these things. In this war, the suspended quotation is a weapon which the author turns on the enemy every so often (the frequency with which the device is used indicates the degree of authorial involvement in this warfare). The Victorian author is decent, and, sensing that the suspended quotation is a weapon, he uses it whenever possible on characters who obviously deserve punishment. There are of course many such characters around in the society the novelist describes: bullies, swaggerers, fakes. Failing one of these, the author can employ the suspended quotation in the disguised aggressiveness of comedy. If no character is around who can be made the butt of an authorial joke, if only good, dignified characters are around, the suspended quotation may be used on one of the good characters. In fact, there will be moments where the novelist feels a particularly strong impulse to interrupt just that good character over there. And so he does, hiding the injury as best he can from both himself and the reader by disguising that injury as solicitude, helpfulness, compassion.

Why should an author make war on characters as a class? Why, more particularly, should Dickens do so? As might be expected, the answer is complex. One important factor here is the social and artistic status of the novelist. The art of fiction has considerably less prestige in the age of Carlyle than it would have in the age of James. In the 1830s, the writer of novels may both be and wish to appear an educated man, a gentleman, and he may find, if he is Dickens, that success in novel-writing gains him not only a great deal of money but invitations to Holland House. Still, a novelist is not a poet or a sage, though his success may bring him the society of sages. At one moment he looks to himself like a Milton or a Carlyle; the next moment, he is a promoted penny-a-liner.[18] One may wish to be rather like the Regency novelists; may (as we have seen) take on some of their airs and mannerisms. The Regency novel was, however, a *roman à clef:* the Regency novelist had to be, or pass for, a member of the fashionable world he described—which is to say, he had to be someone who had social prestige before he took to novel-writing. But such a novelist as Dickens rises through his success in describing the life below. We all remember the history of *Pickwick Papers:* the spectacular, unprecedented triumph came to the author not when he described a prosperous retired grocer (and a retired grocer, of course, was only a *cit*) but when he brought in the cockney Sam Weller.

It is suggestive here to take a very familiar Dickensian locus—the warehouse section of *David Copperfield*—and use it in a new way. Remembering that David is, like his creator, to become a successful novelist and that the book is thus by definition a *Kunstlerroman*, one might read the warehouse passages of the book as a condensed and disguised presentation of the social unease Dickens will come to feel as a novelist, read them as a sort of allegory of the odd relationship Dickens has with his characters. Thus:

> Though perfectly familiar with them [the other boys], my conduct and manner were different enough from theirs to place a space between us. They and the men generally spoke of me as "the little gent," or "the young Suffolker." A certain man named Gregory, who was foreman of the packers, and another named Tipp, who was the carman, and wore a red jacket, used to address me as "David": but I

> think it was mostly when we were very confidential, and when I had made some efforts to entertain them, over our work, with the results of the old readings; which were fast perishing out of my remembrance.
>
> [chap. 9, p. 162]

If we take David's fellow workers to be Dickens's best loved characters, Sam Weller and all those who follow him, the first sentence of this passage becomes a key statement about the style of early Dickensian narrative. If we continue to seek hidden meanings, what follows this statement proves to be quite fascinating. Story telling has to do with remembered readings; it is a genteel accomplishment. But success in this gentlemanly line may lead to one's becoming just "David," and not "the little gent"; may lead to one's inspiring an undesirable familiarity.[19]

Socially, then, the characters who bring Dickens success are potentially embarrassing, and one can see where Dickens might at once be proud of, love, and also rather resent them. But there are more interesting issues relevant to Dickens's use of suspended quotations than complex forms of simple snobbery. If Dickens may have been in some sort embarrassed by the characters who made his fortune (and we might wonder if *Great Expectations* is also an allegorical *Kunstlerroman*) he may also have been jealous of them: and this idea of authorial jealousy is worth exploring.

For the moment I shall let Anthony Trollope be our guide: we are going to be considering the novel in some rather low ways, and here Trollope is invaluable since none of the great Victorian novelists takes a less exalted view of his craft. I shall assume that the sort of thing Trollope says is the sort of thing the others thought about—at least occasionally.

Most of us consider a novel (or a chapter or an installment) as a whole, a pleasing combination of elements in which, if the maker is skillful, variations in texture, pace, subject matter and so forth are at best meaningful and at a minimum pleasing, refreshing, and stimulating for the reader. Trollope does not think of novels and novel-reading in this way. For him, certain things have to be in a novel which are intrinsically boring: a novel is not a symphony with slow and fast movements but a sort of pudding through which the reader spoons his way looking for the currants. It is not just the unsophisticated reader who does this; it is any reader. And the reader is not precisely wrong to do so—that is, Trollope does not believe the batter is really the nobler part of a pudding or that the true delight of a pudding comes with the combined tastes of fruit and batter; the reader is simply a bit unreasonable in wishing for nothing but fruit. An exclusively fruit pudding *would* be nice, and batter is inferior stuff—but a pudding must have batter, and we live in an imperfect world.

The most instructive reflection of the Trollopean attitude—at least the most instructive one I can recall—opens the ninth chapter of *The Duke's Children.* The statement occupies a longish paragraph, but it is a charming paragraph and worth the quoting:

> Perhaps the method of rushing at once "in medias res" is, of all the ways of beginning a story, or a separate branch of a story, the least objectionable. The reader is made to think that the gold lies so near the surface that he will be required to take very little trouble in digging for it. And the writer is enabled—at any rate for a time, and till his neck has become, as it were, warm to the collar,—to throw off from him the difficulties and dangers, the tedium and prolixity, of description. This rushing "in medias res" has doubtless the charm of ease. "Certainly, when I threw her from the garret window to the stony pavement below, I did not anticipate that she would fall so far without injury to life or limb." When a story has been begun after this fashion, without any prelude, without description of the garret or of the pavement or of the lady thrown, or of the speaker, a great amount of trouble seems to have been saved. The mind of the reader fills up the blanks,—if erroneously, still satisfactorily. He knows, at least, that the heroine has encountered a terrible danger, and has escaped from it with almost incredible good fortune; that the

> demon of the piece is a bold demon, not ashamed to speak of his own iniquity, and that the heroine and the demon are so far united that they have been in a garret together. But there is a drawback on the system,—that it is almost impossible to avoid the necessity of doing, sooner or later, that which would naturally be done at first. It answers, perhaps, for half-a-dozen chapters;—and to carry the reader pleasantly for half-a-dozen chapters is a great matter!—but after that a certain nebulous darkness gradually seems to envelope the characters and the incidents. "Is all this going on in the country, or is it in town,—or perhaps in the Colonies? How old was she? Was she tall? Is she fair? Is she heroine-like in her form and gait? And, after all, how high was the garret window?" I have always found that the details would insist on being told at last, and that by rushing "in medias res" I was simply presenting the cart before the horse. But as readers like the cart the best, I will do it once again,—trying it only for a branch of my story,—and will endeavour to let as little as possible of the horse be seen afterwards.

"The difficulties and dangers, the tedium and prolixity, of description": surely one of Trollope's most persistent and endearing tics as storyteller is the indication that something dull must now be discussed.[20]

Assume, then, that this cart-and-horse view of fiction, this sense that parts of any novel must be intrinsically tedious, is not uniquely Trollopean but rather one which Trollope discusses, manifests, with unique forthrightness; assume that all Victorian novelists are aware that at certain moments, in certain chapters, of any fiction the reader is waiting around for something interesting to happen. And, having made these assumptions, take as representative rather than idiosyncratic another Trollopean observation, this one from his *Autobiography:* "the dialogue is generally the most agreeable part of a novel."[21] Recall, then, a more famous statement of the same preference:

> Alice was beginning to get very tired of sitting by her sister on the bank, and of having nothing to do: once or twice she had peeped into the book her sister was reading, but it had no pictures or conversations in it, "and what is the use of a book," thought Alice, "without pictures or conversations?"

We laugh at Alice's forthright question; hypocrite readers, her brothers, we laugh: but we laugh in recognition, and what we recognize is something childlike in our own experience with novels.

Why *should* dialogue be especially attractive to the reader? The answers to this question are varied, curious, and well worth another digression. I'll begin with something already discussed: the facts of the novel as printed language; Victorian layout conventions.

If we think for a moment about that first paragraph of *Alice in Wonderland*, we realize that *peeped* is a significant word there. Alice did not have to read along in her sister's book to discover it was monovocal: she had only to peep into it once or twice. That child is mother to the professor of English. Even now, all grown up, having scribbled on many an index card and stared at many *carte sudate*, even now, as we turn the leaf of a novel, we notice at once whether there is or is not going to be a conversation on the next pages, and if there is to be one, approximately how many speeches it will contain and about how long those speeches will be. We notice these things before we begin to read the words themselves, much as, in reading a book of verse, we notice that distinctive rectangle of print on the next leaf and prepare to experience a sonnet. The difference is that it is meritorious to recognize probable sonnetitude: such recognition means that we will read that poem properly, read it against the background of the European sonnet tradition. It is not meritorious—it is decidedly infra dig—to notice upcoming dialogue: for that recognition leads not to the selection of the proper scholarly backdrop but to an instant of happy, childish expectation: "there's going to be talk; oh *good!*"

We *do* spot the upcoming talk; and the fact that we're able to do so quite easily is an important fact: important in several ways. The marking off of dialogue is, as I wrote earlier, more extravagant in nineteenth-century English fiction than it generally was in the novel of Fielding's age and more punctilious in Victorian fiction than in contemporary French novels. A change of speakers requires a change of paragraph; an inquit must be segregated from the character's words by quotation marks and not mere maid-of-all-work commas. Obviously these nineteenth-century English conventions both testify to and reinforce a sense of the importance of the difference between one voice and another. Putting a still finer point on things, we may say that the modern paragraphing convention places the interchange between characters in distinguished company. Especially when there is a sequence of fairly short speeches, a stretch of dialogue will look rather like a column in a nineteenth-century Bible.[22] A page of dialogue will also look somewhat like a page of verse: both poetry and conversation are more irregular shapes on the page, let more white show through, than expository prose. And it is amusing to think about the resemblance of dialogue to verse: as poetry to the literature of the age, so dialogue to narration within the single book. Like verse, dialogue will tend to be less functional, less informational than the surrounding and contrasting material.[23] Looking at the matter more broadly, we may say that for perfectly obvious economic reasons, unused space on a printed page suggested luxury, elegance, social privilege. (Recall how Sheridan's Sir Benjamin Backbite wished his poems to be printed ". . . on a beautiful quarto page, where a neat rivulet of text shall murmur through a meadow of margin.")[24] And again: cheap editions tended to mean editions with minuscule type and as little blank space as possible.

There is reason, then, to think that the way dialogue was printed in the Victorian age was itself a signal to the reader about the way dialogue ought to be regarded. But Victorian layout convention suggested something else to the reader about dialogue—something that had nothing to do with the way other sorts of texts were printed: it suggested that in reading dialogue the audience would have to do less work than in reading narration.

The more conversation, the less work: that is, incidentally, a bit of Victorian Grub Street wisdom; the hack writer of Dickens's period soon learned that, thanks to the modern paragraphing convention, the more dialogue included in fiction, the better—the more short speeches there are, the more easily an author can fill up a given number of sheets and collect his pay.[25] And, though novelists working for such publishers as Edward Lloyd were more shameless than their more artistic brethren in letting pointless conversations get them through pages quickly, it was not only the lowest of the low who understood the trick and thought of writing conversations as the easier part of their task.[26] But of course that is a producer's, not a consumer's view of fiction: one may reasonably assume that Dickens was aware of the low novelist's wisdom which aligned dialogue with ease and the "solid matter" of narration with hard work, and that this alignment was one of the dozens of things underlying his attitude toward novelistic dialogue; but there is no reason to assume that Dickens's audience knew about such tricks. And surely there is no reason to suppose the Victorian reader, any of those thousands waiting for the next installment of *The Old Curiosity Shop*, thought of reading a Dickens novel as work; surely *that* wonderful view of things came in only with the rise of English as an academic subject.

Yes and no: once again, we do well to assume a certain polyvalence then; and, of course, we can recognize such polyvalence now, in our own experience as readers. Obviously for a Victorian the reading of a Dickens novel was something that contrasted with the work of the day, something that was not work. On the other hand, *any* act of reading was (and to a great extent still is) variously and complexly charged. Reading is a Good Thing, intrinsically praiseworthy. For most of us, the memory of learning to read is our first clear memory of a meritorious intellectual accomplishment. (*David Copperfield* both jogs our self-awareness and testifies to Dickens's in this respect.) For many members of Dickens's first audience, the merit of reading would be stronger still: one knew that the literate rose higher in the world than the illiterate, and one had frequent contact with illiterates, contact which kept one aware that literacy *was* an accomplishment and not to be taken for granted. Thus reading, reading anything, had an aura of merit, as it still does. And complementing this sense of merit is a still more primitive (or fundamental) complacency: we take a certain satisfaction in the completion of any ordered, measured activity: thus, if we finish a "worthless" five-hundred-page book we have less sense that we've wasted our time than we do if we throw that book aside after reading only four hundred pages. And here a consumer's version of Grub Street wisdom is to the point: we at least seem to get through a page of dialogue more quickly than we do a page of description, we are at least liminally aware that there are fewer words to be read on the one page than on the other. But we also assume that one page *counts* as much as another. (Doesn't every page have a number on it?) All pages count equally as steps in a meritorious progression: but some steps are taken more easily than others. When we see that the next page is going to be mostly conversation, we feel again, dimly but deeply, the schoolboy's pleasure in seeing that his next task is an unusually easy one.

These low and primitive pleasures created for us by novelistic layout conventions are things we never discuss, and they are things well worth discussing. Finally, though, they are ancillary: somewhat more familiar subjects of linguistic and critical concern are also somewhat more important.

It has been said that "interaction between narration and dialogue in large measure defines 'fiction' in its broadest sense as a literary type."[27] In the novel of Dickens's age, as perhaps never before, one is aware of this interaction because one is aware of the great gap between the styles of narrative paragraphs and the styles of quoted speech—especially when that speech is most low, captivating, and eccentric. Dickens himself is of course the great example here. (Looking at the matter of eccentric speech eccentrically, looking at it through that *David Copperfield* passage I quoted a bit earlier, we might say that Dickens's desire to "place a space" between author and character "by differences in conduct and manner" becomes, in the parsimony of genius, a source of immense pleasure to the reader. In writing fiction one can not only raise the bridge, one can lower the water; one dissociates oneself from what is low not only by making oneself attractively urbane, but by making the low gloriously, eccentrically, impossibly low.) And underlying the specially powerful marking off of characterly language in Dickens there is that general attractiveness of dialogue which Trollope recognizes and which can exist (as, for instance, in Trollope's own novels) even when the conversing characters do not sound very different from the narrator. Where does this deeper attractiveness come from?

Consider Karl Kroeber's "interaction" again. I think we might compare the effect here to that we find in mixed-media art works. The narrative sections of the novel are like a drawing of an opera box; the words within quotation marks are real ticket stubs and bits of red velvet fastened to that drawing. Dialogue is signified at that level where description is signifier: *that* paragraph was *about* the woman in the room; *this* paragraph *is* the sentence that woman spoke. With dialogue—even the most "artificial" dialogue—we feel we are closer to the room itself, do not have to peer through mediating words to see the things which interest us; thus, in going from a page of narration to a page of dialogue we have a feeling of ease, a sense that we shall now have to expend less imaginative energy;[28] it is (to move from the art museum into the open air) as though we had been bicycling on level ground or a slight uphill slope for ten minutes and then saw that the next stretch of road went gently downhill. Direct quotation allows us to coast, to do less work than we had been doing: and of course the modern layout convention only reinforces this sense that we are moving to an easier stretch of road in moving to a stretch of directly quoted conversation.

This pattern of tension and relaxation, increasing and decreasing immediacy, is always part of narrative. I have brought in the mighty signifier/signified distinction here, but it must be stressed that the sense of the immediacy of dialogue in contrast to narration is by no means something available only to the learned—or so, at least, novelists themselves appear to believe. What I have in mind here is a kind of indirect evidence provided by the way characters (particularly uneducated characters) tell stories in novels. Such tellers of tales have a marked tendency to switch from the past tense to the present when they come to speech-tags and direct quotation: that is, in novels the colloquial storyteller distributes tenses in a way suggesting that a speech directly quoted is more intensely present than a described action. Though there are probably very few imitations of English oral narration in which the present tense is *always* used in tags and *never* in descriptions, it may be taken as a rule that in almost any such imitation composed during the last three centuries, the closer a finite verb is to a direct quotation, the greater its chances of being in the present tense. Eavesdrop the next time you're on a bus and you'll know what sort of usage the novelists drew upon, understood or perhaps misunderstood. (My guess is understood, not misunderstood.) Look at the passages I've collected in Appendix 1 below and at other such novelistic passages. When one considers the way novelists think ordinary folk tell stories, it is difficult not to infer that novelists believe ordinary folk see direct quotation as a privileged part of a tale, the introduction of which works more consistently than anything else does to pull the narrative from past to present.

Very well: we know that the heroine of *Alice in Wonderland* and at least one major Victorian novelist thought conversation either was or tended to be the more attractive component of fiction; we have argued that distribution of tenses in imitated colloquial narration testifies to a sense of the privileged status, the greater vividness of directly quoted speech; we have proposed explanations for what we found, given reasons why direct quotation must by its very nature have advantages over adjacent stretches of description, and we have seen why the advantages of conversation would be greater in the age of Dickens than in other periods. Furthermore, we know that reviewers of Dickens's early novels tended to praise the author for his dialogue—especially the dialogue of his lower-class characters—and either ignore or find fault with the style of his narrative passages[29] —and we know that, deny it though he would, Dickens *did* pay attention to reviews, was only too sensitive to them.[30] Well and good: we assume that Dickens has reason to think his audience is more fond of the dialogue he creates than of the description he creates. What then? Dickens *does* create both things, after all: all credit to him for the batter, and all credit to him for the fruit!

Yes and no. The modern schooled reader tends to be so well drilled in the persona hypothesis ("Even when the narrator does not have a name or a known history, he is a character and *not* to be identified with the creator of the book; his opinions and interpretations are not necessarily correct") or some doctrine even more severe ("Correct interpretation? But what might that be, *mon petit . . .?*") that he forgets how much drilling was needed to bring him to this sophistication. The unschooled reader, however, rather tends to assume the narrator is the author; and thus he tends to forget that the characters are made by the same writer. Here it is hard not to quote a letter John Forster received after the publication of the first volume of his *Life of Dickens*, and which Forster kept, as one learns from his note on the back of it, just because it was so amusing. The letter is from a Mrs. Jane Greene of Dublin, and it concerns her uncle's reading of *The Old Curiosity Shop.* That uncle, writes Mrs. Greene,

> was so *enchanted* with Little Nell that anyone might have supposed she was a *real living* child in whose sad fate he was deeply interested. One evening while silently reading . . . he suddenly sprung from his chair, flung the book violently on the ground, and exclaimed "The Villain! The Rascall!! The bloodthirsty scoundrel!!!" His astonished brother thought he had *gone mad*, and enquired aghast of whom he was speaking? "Dickens," he roared, "he would *commit murder!* He killed my little Nell—He killed my sweet little child!"[31]

We laugh, of course, but again, as with the Alice passage, we laugh in recognition: this is not a bizarre delusion but a common delusion experienced with bizarre intensity. What Mrs. Greene's uncle felt was felt in less extreme form by all those readers who tried to intervene with Dickens on behalf of Little Nell or Little Paul, who tried to influence the author while there was still time; before the next installment was written and the thing settled forever. It is something we still feel—although the characters we most care about and dissociate from their author are not likely to be Nell, Paul, or indeed any of the good characters who die pathetic deaths.

Mrs. Greene's uncle provides us with an extreme example of readerly dissociation of characters and author. But this extreme example is also a useful example because, while one can be sure that letter would have amused Dickens immensely, one can also see that Dickens and Mrs. Greene's uncle have a good deal in common. In his own letters, Dickens very often does sound like a terrorist who has taken a hostage; a hostage personally inoffensive but who must be sacrificed for the cause. Mrs. Greene's uncle and Dickens share assumptions and ideas we have learned to discard. Thus, as Dickens moves toward being villain! rascall!! bloodthirsty scoundrel!!!:

> I am inundated with imploring letters recommending poor little Nell to mercy.
>
> [II, p. 153]
>
> I am slowly murdering the poor child, and grow wretched over it. It wrings my heart. Yet it must be.
>
> [II, p. 180]
>
> Old wounds bleed afresh when I only think of the way of doing it: what the actual doing it will be, God knows.
>
> [II, p. 181]
>
> That Nellicide was the Act of Heaven, as you may see any of these fine mornings when you look about you. If you knew the pain it gave me—but what am I talking of—if you don't know, nobody does.
>
> [II, p. 228]

The uncertain bravado with which that last excerpt ends is

heard more emphatically in Dickens's letter to Forster of 6 December 1846, when the work at hand is *Dombey and Son:* "Paul, I shall slaughter at the end of number five." It is quite of a piece with this that when Dickens discusses his work on a book with an eponymous hero, he falls into the habit of talking about the progress he has made with *him* rather than the progress he has made with *it.*[32]

For both his readers and for Dickens himself, characters in the novels are not simply parts of a work but beings affected by and also affecting the author. Dickens does things to them; they, in turn, like the stars of hit television series, can bring popularity to the work in which they appear and can also reduce that work's popularity by leaving. Sam Weller's services to his master Dickens were greater than those to his master Pickwick; Dickens may "slaughter" Paul, but when Paul goes he takes a good part of the audience with him.[33]

Sam Weller is to Dickens what yellow hair is to Anne Gregory. Dickens, the Dickens of the early and middle years especially, knew he was an immensely entertaining fellow, and wanted everyone else to know it. And all people did know—knew it part of the time, knew it when they thought hard and coolly about the matter. And yet there was always that other sense of the matter, the sense that the urbanely elegant (and perhaps too elegant, perhaps a touch vulgar) Dickens was a kind of manager for these vigorously or comically or pathetically low characters, was a sort of middleman.

The problem was that Dickens wanted to be not just the great imitator but the Inimitable; England's second Shakespeare was not the chameleon poet but the peacock poet. And sometimes he does spread his feathers oddly. Consider for a moment some quite early Dickens; a paragraph from the second chapter of *Oliver Twist* in which the author uses an oft-told joke as part of his attack upon the new Poor Law:

> Everybody knows the story of another experimental philosopher who had a great theory about a horse being able to live without eating, and who demonstrated it so well, that he got his own horse down to a straw a day, and would un-

questionably have rendered him a very spirited and rampacious animal on nothing at all, if he had not died, four-and-twenty hours before he was to have had his first comfortable bait of air.

[p. 4]

Terrible! This is, as Dickens says, a story everybody knows; but has anyone ever heard it told worse? We are spared "graminivorous quadruped," but, especially as he moves toward the punch line, Dickens misses few other opportunities to ruin his joke with little embellishments and humorous elegancies. Surely Dickens knows how to tell a simple joke better than this! Of course; the root of the trouble lies in the opening, "Everybody knows the story." It is not that Dickens is characteristically unwilling to repeat—he knows the good will kept up by the recognition of an old semiproverbial joke. The trouble is that he cannot resist the impulse to signal "look at *me* tell that old joke." And so the joke comes to resemble a Gershwin song worked up for a Las Vegas show.

If we turn back a few pages and look at the first chapter of *Oliver Twist* we will find things rather like that poor, bespangled, plume-covered little joke. Certain allowances should be made: Dickens *is* very young as he writes these pages; he is known primarily for his humor, and chapter 1 of *Oliver Twist* is to be fundamentally pathetic. Still, all exceptions excepted, listen to the strain, the verbal lapel-grabbing, in the third paragraph of that novel:

Although I am not disposed to maintain that the being born in a workhouse, is in itself the most fortunate and enviable circumstance that can possibly befall a human being, I do mean to say that in this particular instance, it was the best thing for Oliver Twist that could by possibility have occurred. The fact is, that there was considerable difficulty in inducing Oliver to take upon himself the office of respiration—a troublesome practice, but one which custom has rendered necessary to our easy existence; and for some time he lay gasping on a little flock mattress, rather unequally poised between this world and the next: the balance being

> decidedly in favour of the latter. Now, if during this brief period, Oliver had been surrounded by careful grandmothers, anxious aunts, experienced nurses, and doctors of profound wisdom, he would most inevitably and indubitably have been killed in no time. There being nobody by, however, but an old pauper woman, who was rendered rather misty by an unwonted allowance of beer; and a parish surgeon who did matters by contract; Oliver and Nature fought out the point between them. The result was, that, after a few struggles, Oliver breathed, sneezed, and proceeded to advertise to the inmates of the workhouse the fact of a new burden having been imposed upon the parish, by setting up as loud a cry as could reasonably have been expected from a male infant who had not been possessed of that very useful appendage, a voice, for a much longer space of time than three minutes and a quarter.

This is a paragraph at war with itself, the paragraph of a young writer who wants his readers to sympathize with sympathetic characters and detest detestable ideas and institutions—but also the paragraph of a writer who wants to charm his audience and win them *to himself* in a Harold Skimpole sort of way. (Notice the Skimpolean ploy. It is whimsically demonstrated that what seemed to be much for the worse has in fact turned out to be for the best: Oliver lives rather than dies, Coavenes has employment and an income.)[34] The paragraph moves not with the struggle between Nature and Oliver but with the struggle between Dickens's wish to say "look at that!" and his wish to say "look at me!" Through his early and middle years—that is, during the period in which he wrote his most widely loved novels—Dickens the novelist was (deeply if obscurely) a jealous god, not wanting admiration for his creatures to becloud or weaken or replace admiration for the creator. And that jealousy is something not only deeply if obscurely felt by the writer but deeply if obscurely felt by the reader; it is in fact connected with the special affection Old Persuasion Dickensians felt for those early and middle novels, and their comparative coolness toward the late darker works.

Here, then, is an important context in which to place this particular writer's fondness for suspended quotations. Charles Dickens has a strong sense of himself as the narrator of his fictions and of the named characters in those works as *not* himself, less truly himself than is his narrating voice. Socially, this separation may have been a comfortable thing for Dickens—reassuring to Dickens in his "little gent" aspect. But the Charles Dickens who was intermittently and trivially a snob was deeply and always an egotist: and as an egotist, he is vexed by the thought that it is really Sam Weller and Micawber and Little Nell whom everyone loves—that, as we now say, those characters *make* the books in which they appear (and which, stars that they are, they can leave for guest appearances in pirated stage versions, toby mugs, gimcracks!). Dickens is, in short, jealous of the characters he has created, and one place this jealousy shows up is in the interruptions which spoil or weaken the intended effects of speeches made by those characters—such speeches being irritatingly privileged parts of books, the things belonging to characters which fickle readers like better than even the most whimsical and urbane authorial description.

At the root of this writer's exceptionally strong liking for suspended quotations is authorial jealousy: an impulse to seize, to mar, the special advantages enjoyed by characters, those minions of fortune and worms of the hour. This is our central hypothesis; and it is a hypothesis which allows one to make new kinds of sense out of some well-known facts of Dickens's life and art.

The life, to start with. In the Victorian age there still exist two sorts of semantic overlap which will be familiar to anyone who has dealt with medieval culture, but probably not so familiar to those whose interests are exclusively modern. First, *to write* suggests both to be an author and to be a drudge, a copyist. In an age which requires a great deal of hand-copying, which has the printing press but not the typewriter, tape recorder, or xerox machine, writing suggests ancillary as much as it does primary, creative labor. The ambiguity here is of course the one Melville plays upon in *Bartleby the Scriv-*

*ener* and one whose importance in *Bleak House*, for instance, is well worth considering. The second is the connection between *story* and *history*: there is a pale, pervasive amusement in nineteenth-century novels concerning what had been, not many years before, a still intermittently serious tradition of trying to pass off works of fiction as factual reports. *The compiler of this history . . . ; this chronicle would not be complete without . . .:* The reader of Victorian novels knows the pleasantry well enough and smiles at it, understanding that it implies a sort of scribelike, deferential attitude taken by the "creative" writer toward his creation; it is the joke we find in the very first paragraph of the novel whose full title is *The Posthumous Papers of the Pickwick Club.* The author is at best a diligent compiler:

> The first ray of light which illumines the gloom, and converts into a dazzling brilliancy that obscurity in which the earlier history of the public career of the immortal Pickwick would appear to be involved, is derived from the perusal of the following entry in the Transactions of the Pickwick Club, which the editor of these papers feels the highest pleasure in laying before his readers, as a proof of the careful attention, indefatigable assiduity, and nice discrimination, with which his search of the multifarious documents confided to him has been conducted.

What makes this sort of pleasantry especially noteworthy in the case of Dickens is that for him it is not merely an inheritance from earlier novelists; Dickens did begin as a writer in the humbler sense of the word. He started by making verbatim transcriptions of the spoken word rather than of documents; in short, the great novelist began as a humble recorder of speech. Following his father's example, young Dickens decided to become a newspaper parliamentary reporter and, since a parliamentary reporter had to be able to take down speeches accurately, he set out to teach himself the (by modern standards) exceedingly difficult Gurney system of shorthand. The story of all this—the young man's tenacity and his success while still in his teens—is well told by Forster, and there is, of course, the fictionalized version of the experience in *David Copperfield*. One fine paragraph from the latter certainly ought to be considered here (I italicize the words which seem to me especially revealing):

> I bought an approved scheme of the noble art and mystery of stenography (which cost me ten and sixpence), and plunged into a sea of perplexity that brought me, in a few weeks, to the confines of distraction. The changes that were rung upon dots, which in such a position meant such a thing, and in such another position something else, entirely different; the wonderful vagaries that were played by circles; the unaccountable consequences that resulted from marks like flies' legs; the tremendous effects of a curve in a wrong place; not only troubled my waking hours, but reappeared before me in my sleep. When I had groped my way, blindly, through these difficulties, and had mastered the alphabet, which was an Egyptian Temple in itself, *there then appeared a procession of new horrors, called arbitrary characters; the most despotic characters I have ever known;* who *insisted*, for instance, that a thing like the beginning of a cobweb, meant expectation, and that a pen-and-ink sky-rocket stood for disadvantageous. When I had fixed these wretches in my mind, I found that they had driven everything else out of it.
>
> [chap. 38, p. 545]

"Arbitrary *characters*" is delightful, but I shall do no more than draw attention to that happy pun or accident, pat it on the head, and pass it by. What really concerns me here is the political turn the imagery takes, the *despotic* nature of those characters. The shorthand itself is a tyranny to which one submits, but for Dickens submitting oneself to these arbitrary characters was merely preparation for close exposure to genuinely political arbitrary characters: parliament, for most of whose members the young man now developed a permanent contempt, but the *ipsissima verba* of whose members and would-be members he now had to record, wherever, whenever, and at whatever speed they were uttered. Here I quote from remarks Dickens made in 1865 at the second annual dinner of the Newspaper Press Fund:

> I hold a brief to-night for my brothers. I went into the gallery of the House of Commons as a parliamentary reporter when I was a boy, and I left it—I can hardly believe the inexorable truth—nigh thirty years ago. I have pursued the calling of a reporter under circumstances of which many of my brethren here can form no adequate conception. I have often transcribed for the printer, from my shorthand notes, important public speeches in which the strictest accuracy was required, and a mistake in which would have been to a young man severely compromising, writing on the palm of my hand, by the light of a dark lantern, in a post-chaise and four; galloping through a wild country, and through the dead of the night, at the then surprising rate of fifteen miles an hour. The very last time I was at Exeter, I strolled through the castle-yard there to identify, for the amusement of a friend, the spot on which I once "took," as we used to call it, an election speech of Lord John Russell at the Devon contest, in the midst of a lively fight maintained by all the vagabonds in that division of the county, and under such a pelting rain, that I remember two good-natured colleagues who chanced to be at leisure held a pocket-handkerchief over my notebook, after the manner of a state canopy in an ecclesiastical procession. I have worn my knees by writing on them on the old back-row of the old gallery of the old House of Commons; and I have worn my feet by standing to write in a preposterous pen in the old House of Lords, where we used to be huddled together like so many sheep—kept in waiting, say, until the Woolsack might want re-stuffing.[35]

Of shorthand Dickens remarks to those at the dinner, "The pleasure that I used to feel in the rapidity and dexterity of its exercise has never faded out of my breast," and the reports that have come down to us confirm that Dickens was an excellent stenographer. But again, if we turn to the *David Copperfield* version of this part of Dickens's experience, we find a memorable description of David's humiliation the first time he tried to take down the words of one of the master orators at Doctors' Commons: "Shall I ever forget how the crack speaker walked off from me before I began, and left my imbecile pencil staggering about the paper as if it were in a fit" [p. 545]. Logically, shorthand and fatuous public speech are first humiliating tyrannies and later, when one plays skillfully by their rules, things which help one to rise in the world; psychologically, in memory, the sense of humiliation and the sense of accomplishment share a berth.

Before Dickens becomes a writer in sense B—before he becomes Boz, the Inimitable—he becomes a writer in sense A, a maker of copies. In both cases he is valued, is a success, in large part because of the words of others (real or imaginary) which he transmits to the public. But how nice, after that self-training to keep up with public blather, after the waiting for speakers in inconvenient places, after the humiliations inflicted by crack speakers—how nice to be able to interrupt the speaker at will and to be able, with the catchword suspension, to force the crack speaker to start over again.[36]

While thinking about Dickens's life, we ought to take a few minutes to consider two phantasy careers which were dear to him: acting and periodical editing. In fact, it might be better to call these subordinate careers or curtailed careers rather than phantasy ones, since Dickens did put a considerable amount of time and energy into the attempts to be both novelist and editor, novelist and actor—and indeed he was fairly successful as both editor and actor.

The story of Dickens and the stage has been told often, and here we have no reason to treat his various private theatricals and reading tours in any detail; it is enough to see the obvious: Charles Dickens as actor, as reader from his own works, in after-dinner speeches, greatly enjoyed having an audience *right there*, looking at *him*. But one thing we might consider more closely is a kind of dramatic entertainment which enjoyed its greatest popularity during the years when suspended quotations luxuriated and multiplied. This entertainment was known—magnificently—as the monopolylogue.[37]

The monopolylogue is basically the kind of performance we still find from time to time in Peter Sellers or Alastair Sim movies: one actor plays a number of different characters. The early Victorian fashion for such performances (which are, of course, more difficult, more difficult and exhilarating, when done live than when done for the camera, since the stage actor must be able to change both personalities and costumes with great speed) was started by Charles Matthews, the actor the young Charles Dickens most admired. From the 1810s on, Matthews became especially famous for his "At Homes"—entertainments in which he would play dozens of different parts in the course of an evening. The interesting thing about this sort of performance is that in it the virtuoso actor is not for a moment forgotten by the audience: that is, we're never very deeply engaged with poor Desdemona up there but always thinking about how remarkable it is that Mr. X can be so much like Desdemona, and like Iago, and like Cassio, and possibly like the handkerchief. The monopolylogue is, one might say, Bottom's other dream, the ideal form for an egomaniacal actor. (Victorian drama generally was, as Philip Collins reminds us, a drama for virtuosos, single stars;[38] in this sense the monopolylogue might be thought of as the most characteristic expression of Victorian dramatic taste.) It is amusing to play with the relation between the monopolylogue and various forms of Victorian high literary art: if one thinks of Browning as a sort of monopolylogist, for instance, one sees why it is so difficult for some of us to enter deeply into the emotions and dilemmas of those various *dramatis personae;* we keep hearing Browning's "look at *me!* look at all the things I can do!" More to the point, we might hold on to the formula, "as monopolylogue to regular drama, so suspended quotation to normal novelistic dialogue": in both monopolylogue and suspended quotation, the artist—actor or author—gives his audience less than their usual opportunity to forget the creator in their admiration for the creatures. Certainly it is worth noting that during the years when the monopolylogue was most popular in England, Dickens and Mark Lemon collaborated on the farce *Mr. Nightingale's Diary*, in which Dickens got to play six different roles. In this farce it is important that the audience *not* know in advance of the monopolylogish stunt, and, as Edgar Johnson describes it, "The second-night audience screamed with laughter at this piece, and were flabbergasted near the end to discover that Dickens in rapid succession had disguised himself to play . . . a lawyer, a Sam Wellerish waiter, a maniacally enthusiastic walker, a hypochondriac, a gabbling Sairey Gamplike old woman, and a deaf sexton."[39] One imagines a great sweetness for Dickens in that flabbergasting; it is easy to understand that performance as a ritual rectification of the successful novelist's relation with his audience, who tend to forget that if they love Sam Weller and Sarah Gamp, they really ought to be loving Charles Dickens. It is a moment a jealous god might dream up—if we can imagine a jealous god with a sense of humor.

Dickens's second secondary career is in journalism: not the journalism of the penny-a-liner or the parliamentary reporter anymore, but that of editor in a Victorian adaptation/continuation of the eighteenth-century belletristic periodical. However successful his novels, Dickens always has the Goldsmithian *Bee* in his bonnet, the wish to control something like *Master Humphrey's Clock* or *All the Year Round* or *Household Words:* a publication in which installments of some new Dickensian novel would be no more than one attraction among others. There is, of course, much that lies behind such an ambition. Dickens always liked the idea of more money. More important, the sort of egotism and aggressiveness we have been seeking within Dickens's novels always enjoyed a most vigorous and various existence outside of them, and, as John Sutherland has put it in *Victorian Novelists and Publishers*, "Dickens' career, viewed from one aspect, emerges as a successful elbowing aside of the booksellers who stood between him and the reader."[40] To edit is to control, and Dickens liked to control; he was, in F. W. Dupee's words, "the artist as tycoon."[41] But what particularly concerns us here is that matter of the yellow hair. Consider a lovely paragraph from Forster's *Life*, in which he tells us of

Dickens's attempts to find just the right name for a new periodical:

> The title took some time and occupied many letters. One of the first thought-of has now the curious interest of having foreshadowed, by the motto proposed to accompany it, the title of the series of *All the Year Round* which he was led to substitute for the older series in 1859. "THE ROBIN. With this motto from Goldsmith. *The redbreast, celebrated for its affection to mankind, continues with us, the year round.*" That however was rejected. Then came: "MANKIND. This I think very good." It followed the other nevertheless. After it came: "And here a strange idea, but with decided advantages. 'CHARLES DICKENS. A weekly journal designed for the instruction and entertainment of all classes of readers. CONDUCTED BY HIMSELF.'" Still something was wanting in that also. Next day there arrived: "I really think if there *be* anything wanting in the other name, that this is very pretty, and just supplies it. THE HOUSEHOLD VOICE. I have thought of many others, as—THE HOUSEHOLD GUEST. THE HOUSEHOLD FACE. THE COMRADE. THE MICROSCOPE. THE HIGHWAY OF LIFE. THE LEVER. THE ROLLING YEARS. THE HOLLY TREE (with two lines from Southey for a motto). EVERYTHING. But I rather think the VOICE is it." It was near indeed; but the following day came, "HOUSEHOLD WORDS. This is a very pretty name": and the choice was made.
>
> [VI.4, vol. 2, pp. 65-66]

The splendid thing here of course is that rejected title, CHARLES DICKENS—a title especially magnificent because it comes right after MANKIND. Dickens did settle at last for HOUSEHOLD WORDS as the name and "Conducted by Charles Dickens" as merely one of four lines on each masthead. But the real title, the secret name, of all those periodicals is surely "CHARLES DICKENS. A journal designed for the instruction and entertainment of all classes of readers. CONDUCTED BY HIMSELF."

What the running of a periodical offered to Dickens was the possibility of testing, basking in, the public's unmediated love of Charles Dickens. They would not be buying issues of *Pickwick Papers* because Sam Weller appeared in them; they would not be buying issues of a particular journal because a particular novel was being serialized in it: they would be eager to buy a miscellany because it would be "conducted by Charles Dickens," because, as for a blissful moment really seemed possible, it would *be* CHARLES DICKENS. Behind all of this, as I've suggested, lies the eighteenth-century and Regency idea of the periodical essay, in which manner, the personality of the writer, was far more important than matter, and we tried the roast pig because we knew it was Lamb. "Trust *me;* love *me: I* will entertain and instruct you; allow *me* to choose the good things I shall lay before you in profusion."

While on the subject of urbane and charming narrators, we might consider a correlation between the period (and especially Dickensian) taste for suspended quotations and the period (and especially Dickensian) taste for comically pompous language: too fancy syntax, Latinate diction. For us, the importance of this fashion lies in the fact that Victorian polysyllabic humor is always polyvalent. As G. W. Turner puts it, the mannerism allows the writer to have it both ways—to use and also to mock learned vocabulary and sounding rhythms.[42] Modern critics tend to stress the satire; but the more educated reviewers of the period seem to have taken the satiric intent of such language no more seriously than we take the satiric intent of yet one more spoof of the traditional spy or cowboy movie. Such reviewers saw cockney gaudiness in the device, the frippery of the half-educated, imperfectly civilized. Furthermore, someone like Dickens, who knew the lower strata of journalism, would have associated the style with the humiliating daily scramble to gain just a little more money. He would have known the comic Latinate style as the resource of those least powerful and most desperate authors, the penny-a-liners who used this style so that their articles would be a few lines longer and they a few pennies richer.[43] For Dickens the ornate polysyllabic style was variously meretricious, and best introduced with some aura of satire about it; on the other hand, the style was also very attractive—something he *wanted* to sneak in.

Now if we assume that when Dickens uses such diction it is not in most cases his primary purpose to give us precisely aimed rapier thrusts of satire, but rather that he does indeed use satire as a sort of cover to indulge a somewhat shameful taste, we may well wonder why he was so attracted to this esthetically, socially, and economically suspect diction. The answer is, essentially, that the arch polysyllabic style was the only one Dickens possessed which would do certain things: first, it *does* create a barrier of words, an insulating layer between the events described and the audience. Dickens at certain moments knows that language ought not to insulate; but again and again we find him doing for us what Micawber does for himself. Thus, for instance, this passage from *The Old Curiosity Shop:*

> Daniel Quilp, who was not much affected by a bright morning save in so far as it spared him the trouble of carrying an umbrella, caused himself to be put ashore hard by the wharf, and proceeded thither,—through a narrow lane which, partaking of the amphibious character of its frequenters, had as much water as mud in its composition, and a very liberal supply of both. Arrived at his destination, the first object that presented itself to his view was a pair of very imperfectly shod feet elevated in the air with the soles upward, which remarkable appearance was referable to the boy, who being of an eccentric spirit and having a natural taste for tumbling was now standing on his head and contemplating the aspect of the river under these uncommon circumstances. He was speedily brought on his heels by the sound of his master's voice, and as soon as his head was in its right position, Mr. Quilp, to speak expressively in the absence of a better verb, "punched it" for him.
>
> [chap. 5, p. 41]

It must be stressed that neither of the characters described—neither Quilp nor the boy—pretends to a style at all like the style of this passage. The language here is the functional equivalent of the pastels Wrayburn uses to fumigate the room when Mr. Dolls has been present. Very odd. This would seem a formula for novelistic disaster: why does Dickens want to insulate his readers from the things being described? Not, I think, because of any interest in novelistic reflexivity. No, it is first of all because he wants to flatter his audience: he can use, and they can understand, language which would *not* be comprehensible to Quilp and Quilp's boy: the presentation of these characters both amuses in itself and appeals to one's *amour-propre* by reminding one of how far below one this all is. (Again: the bridge is raised and the water is lowered.) But the flattery of the reader is accomplished in other ways also. Charles Dickens—Dickens as narrator—is competing with these characters rather as one actor competes with others. Quilp is all disconcerting tricks—eats, drinks, appears in ways that catch the attention, distract us from whatever else is going on. And just here, in the passage quoted, that boy—well, imagine for a moment how one of the stars in a play would react if he found that there on stage with him was a bit-player *standing on his head.* Dickens knows about scene-stealing, elbowing others out of the way, whether those others are publishers or characters. But Dickens is hardly going to stand on his head or eat eggs in the shell. What he does instead is exploit the advantages he has over those characters, the advantages not of "natural" eloquence but of ornate, genteel eloquence. He too will amuse—but in a classy way. He will do for us what the characters cannot do: make us feel socially superior, urbane.

This sounds rather snobbish, and of course the ornate polysyllabic mode *is* snobbish, a flaunting of linguistic status symbols. The nineteenth-century reviewers who objected to such prose were closer to the truth than the twentieth-century critics who see passages in this style as sharply focused satire. And I must say that—in my case, anyway—the thing does work, at least some of the time: when in *Great Expectations* the mature Pip tells us how Mrs. Joe hurled his younger self at her husband, and adds "I often served as a connubial missile" [p. 7] I am delighted, but know that my delight in this language is a form of self-love, a congratulating of myself on understanding the Latinate phrase. Yet there is something here—as there is something in the suspended quotation—deeper than an appeal to snobbery: there is the felt presence of a need for attention and love, a need so deep that it will resort to anything—interruptions of speeches, conspicuously (and therefore brassily, shrilly) prestigious language—to gain our attention. In both the interruptions of speech and the "pointlessly" ornate diction we feel Dickens's deep desire to win us not to this book but to himself.

We return now both to dialogue itself, and yet once more to that most important change between earlier and modern novelistic paragraphing conventions. What I want to consider here, though, is a new question about the change: the way it affects the phenomenon of tagging, transforms it, in certain very common situations, from a necessity to an option. To illustrate what I mean, I shall quote a fairly long exchange from *Tom Jones*—part of the conversation between Jones and Square after Square is found with Molly—presented (as it was in the eighteenth-century editions) in a single paragraph. Thus:

> 'Well reasoned, old Boy,' answered *Jones;* 'but why dost thou think that I should desire to expose thee? I promise thee, I was never better pleased with thee in my Life; and unless thou hast a Mind to discover it thyself, this Affair may remain a profound Secret for me.' 'Nay, Mr. *Jones,*' replied *Square,* 'I would not be thought to undervalue Reputation. Good Fame is a Species of the KALON, and it is by no means fitting to neglect it. Besides, to murder one's own Reputation is a kind of Suicide, a detestable and odious Vice. If you think proper, therefore, to conceal any Infirmity of mine; (for such I may have, since no man is perfect;) I promise you I will not betray myself. Things may be fitting to be done, which are not fitting to be boasted of; for by

the perverse Judgment of the World, That often becomes the Subject of Censure, which is, in Truth, not only innocent but laudable.' 'Right!' cries *Jones*, 'what can be more innocent than the Indulgence of a natural Appetite? or what more laudable than the Propagation of our Species?' 'To be serious with you,' answered *Square*, 'I profess they always appeared so to me.' 'And yet,' said *Jones*, 'you was of a different Opinion, when my Affair with this Girl was first discovered.' 'Why, I must confess,' says *Square*, 'as the Matter was misrepresented to me by that Parson *Thwackum*, I might condemn the Corruption of Innocence: It was that, Sir, it was that—and that—: For you must know, Mr. *Jones*, in the Consideration of Fitness, very minute Circumstances, Sir, very minute circumstances cause great Alteration.'— 'Well,' cries *Jones*, 'be that as it will, it shall be your own Fault, as I have promised you, if you ever hear any more of this Adventure. Behave kindly to the Girl, and I will never open my Lips concerning the Matter to any one. And, *Molly*, do you be faithful to your Friend, and I will not only forgive your Infidelity to me, but will do you all the Service I can.' So saying, he took a hasty Leave, and slipping down the Ladder retired with much Expedition.

[V, chap. 5, pp. 176–77]

What we have here is of course a new tag every time there is a change of speakers. This is virtually standard in *Tom Jones* and earlier works as well—and virtually standard for good reasons. For notice what happens when one takes this single-paragraph duologue[44] and separates the speeches with dashes and quotation marks but leaves out all but the first tag:

"Well reasoned, old Boy," answered *Jones;* "but why dost thou think that I should desire to expose thee? I promise thee, I was never better pleased with thee in my Life; and unless thou hast a Mind to discover it thyself, this Affair may remain a profound Secret for me."—"Nay, Mr. *Jones*, I would not be thought to undervalue Reputation. Good Fame is a Species of the KALON, and it is by no means fitting to neglect it. Besides, to murder one's own Reputation is a

> kind of Suicide, a detestable and odious Vice. If you think proper, therefore, to conceal any Infirmity of mine; (for such I may have, since no man is perfect;) I promise you I will not betray myself. Things may be fitting to be done, which are not fitting to be boasted of; for by the perverse Judgment of the World, That often becomes the Subject of Censure, which is, in Truth, not only innocent but laudable."—"Right! what can be more innocent than the Indulgence of a natural Appetite? or what more laudable than the Propagation of our Species?"—"To be serious with you, I profess they always appeared so to me."—"And yet you was of a different Opinion, when my Affair with this Girl was first discovered."—"Why I must confess, as the Matter was misrepresented to me by that Parson *Thwackum*, I might condemn the Corruption of Innocence: It was that, Sir, it was that—and that—: For you must know, Mr. *Jones*, in the Consideration of Fitness, very minute Circumstances, Sir, very minute Circumstances cause great Alteration."—"Well, be that as it will, it shall be your own Fault, as I have promised you, if you ever hear any more of this Adventure. Behave kindly to the Girl, and I will never open my Lips concerning the Matter to any one. And, *Molly*, do you be faithful to your Friend, and I will not only forgive your Infidelity to me, but will do you all the Service I can." So saying, he took a hasty Leave, and slipping down the Ladder retired with much Expedition.

One does get lost after a while, despite the fact that there are only two speakers, and the conversation is not a strikingly disconnected one. On the other hand, if you try the experiment of writing out this second version of the conversation according to the new paragraphing convention—that is, marking each Jones-to-Square or Square-to-Jones switch with a new paragraph—you will find that it is perfectly easy to follow the characters' talk. We see then one reason why the general acceptance of that new paragraphing convention is the great event in our small area of English stylistic history. In duologues almost always, and frequently in more complex interchanges, tagging became optional rather than necessary—which is to say, tagging of any kind became (under any definition) a matter of style.

One response to the new possibility of freedom from tags is to exploit it as much as possible—that is, to develop a sense of how often a reader really needs or would appreciate a speaker-identification and avoid tags in other places. When he writes *Waverley*, Walter Scott seems to use tags for only about 60 percent of the speeches,[45] and one finds whole pages of duologue where there is not one word of narrative—not one word, that is, outside quotation marks. In *Emma*, Jane Austen seems to favor a similar mixture: about 40 percent of the speeches are untagged. With Austen, too, it is a familiar part—indeed, a particularly valued part—of the reader's experience to be left completely alone with the characters for a page or two, or through such exchanges as:

> "I dare say your apologies were accepted, sir. Mr. Elton knows you."
>
> "Yes; but a young lady—a bride—I ought to have paid my respects to her if possible. It was being very deficient."
>
> "But, my dear papa, you are no friend to matrimony; and therefore why should you be so anxious to pay your respects to a *bride?* It ought to be no recommendation to *you.* It is encouraging people to marry if you make so much of them."
>
> "No, my dear, I never encouraged anybody to marry, but I would always wish to pay every proper attention to a lady—and a bride, especially, is never to be neglected. More is avowedly due to *her.* A bride, you know, my dear, is always the first in company, let the others be who they may."
>
> "Well, papa, if this is not encouragement to marry, I do not know what is. And I should never have expected you to be lending your sanction to such vanity-baits for young ladies."
>
> "My dear, you do not understand me. This is a matter of mere common politeness and good-breeding, and has nothing to do with any encouragement of people to marry."
>
> [*Emma*, chap. 14, p. 190]

For both Scott and Austen (and indeed for a good number of later novelists as well) the simpler tags—"said she," "he replied," are informative signs on a scenic road: it's nice to use them only when necessary and thereby allow the reader as nearly an unobstructed view as possible. Dickens's employment of the new paragraphing convention and of such minimally informative tags is, however, considerably more complex. It is clear, as early as *Pickwick Papers,* that he is aware of expressive possibilities here. Consider, for instance, the following exchange, which you, reader, are in a particularly good position to appreciate, since what you hold in your hand is not a low-priced reprint of all *The Posthumous Papers of the Pickwick Club* but that decidedly expensive commodity, a scholarly monograph:

> "Now, gen'l'm'n," said the hostler, "coach is ready, if you please."
> "Is all my luggage in?" inquired Mr. Magus.
> "All right, sir."
> "Is the red bag in?"
> "All right, sir."
> "And the striped bag?"
> "Fore boot, sir."
> "And the brown-paper parcel?"
> "Under the seat, sir."
> "And the leather hat-box?"
> "They're all in, sir."
> "Now will you get up?" said Mr. Pickwick.
> [chap. 22, p. 300]

Now at the heart of the joke here is a clash between two rules for paragraphing: Rule 1, a change of speakers calls for a new paragraph; Rule 2, a change of paragraph announces the introduction of a new and noteworthy topic of discussion. Of those concerned—author, readers, characters—only Mr. Magus would believe both rules have been observed throughout. But there is a second sort of mimetic play in these lines which involves a flagrant use of the Grub Street writer's trick I discussed earlier. The mimesis here depends on the venerable principle that time is money: in this case it is the reader's money which is involved and Mr. Pickwick's time. Magus delays Pickwick and the other characters by demanding that his questions all be satisfactorily answered before the coach departs. The reader knows that he has bought and is now reading an issue of a serial publication. That issue is uniform in size with the earlier ones he has bought and read: he has purchased so many pages in such a size type of such a length filled with prose about the Pickwickians. But he has not actually purchased a certain number of *words* about the Pickwickians, and he has tacitly agreed to certain conventions which allow certain lines to remain largely blank. There is the loophole—there Magus/Dickens can cheat him and make him feel a frustration comparable to that felt by Pickwick. And of course the absence of tags here only makes the cheating more obvious.

Now the Magus passage shows us that from the very beginning of his career as a novelist, Dickens knows how to exploit our mixed and contradictory feelings about the experience of reading and about the privileged status of dialogue. Just now, though, I want to emphasize a simpler point. While Dickens obviously knows that it is possible, in many situations, to present stretches of untagged dialogue without bewildering the reader, and while he does use the new speaker/new paragraph rule, he is, at this time, far more reluctant to use untagged speeches than is either Scott or Austen. In *Pickwick* only about six out of one hundred speeches will be left untagged, and there will be even fewer untagged quotations in *Oliver Twist*, *Nicholas Nickleby*, and *Dombey*.[46] During the first half of his career we shall not find Dickens leaving much more than one speech in ten untagged.

Though not unique, the heavy use of tagging is certainly a striking feature of Dickens's early style, setting Dickensian fiction in contrast not only with fiction by Austen and Scott but with such contemporary works as *Jane Eyre* (about 56 percent untagged), Kingsley's *Yeast* (about 60 percent untagged) and Gaskell's *Mary Barton* (about 45 percent untagged). Why is Dickens so reluctant to do without tags? Not, I think, because of that interest in suprasegmentals; the suprasegmentals are there, of course, but look through an early Dickens novel and you'll find there is usually a great deal more tagging in duologues than there is information about gestures and tone. No, that heavy use of tags is far better explained by the principle *inquit, ergo sum:* unlike Austen, Dickens does not *want* to disappear from the drawing room for several pages at a time and leave his readers alone with the characters. That freedom the New Convention novelists enjoy is for the younger Dickens a most unappealing freedom, and he keeps finding excuses to stay in the room and remind us of his presence: good excuses, sometimes (an expressive suprasegmental) and if a good excuse isn't to hand, a bad excuse, a bare "said he" or "she replied." A most unappealing freedom, a threatening freedom: for—what if we discover we can get on quite well without Boz, that most charming and hardworking of cicerones? What if we find we have learned the language and know the local customs and can deal with the natives by ourselves? That must not be; we must not be allowed to stumble into a situation where we might make such a discovery. "He said": this is not information but a pseudoattention, the brushing away of an imaginary doubt as if it were an imaginary bit of soot on our clothing. "He said": it is a phatic gesture, the equivalent of "lovely weather we've been having" in casual conversation; it means "here I am, here you are: there is a relation between us."[47]

This overattentiveness of the cicerone is something we are particularly aware of when Dickens is being sentimental: we recognize the tug at the heartstrings for what it is long before we recognize the tug at the sleeve:

> "My Kate," said the lady, whose voice was serious, but very calm and sweet, and had so impressed Florence from the first moment of her hearing it, "of all the youthful people here, you are her natural and harmless friend. . . ."
> [*Dombey*, chap. 24, p. 346]

We hate such things and rather congratulate ourselves for hating them: certainly we are quite aware of authorial manipulation as we read such a passage. But consider, for a moment, the following sort of passage, in which Dickens is being perfectly enjoyable and not at all sentimental. And as you read consider how different this would have seemed if Jane Austen had been asked to edit it:

> "Then mind you recollect, and do as I tell you," said Mrs. Kenwigs. "Shall Mr. Johnson begin, uncle?"
>
> "I am ready to hear, if Mr. Johnson is ready to commence, my dear," said the collector, assuming the air of a profound critic. "What sort of language do you consider French, sir?"
>
> "How do you mean?" asked Nicholas.
>
> "Do you consider it a good language, sir?" said the collector; "a pretty language, a sensible language?"
>
> "A pretty language, certainly," replied Nicholas; "and as it has a name for everything, and admits of elegant conversation about everything, I presume it is a sensible one."
>
> "I don't know," said Mr. Lillyvick, doubtfully. "Do you call it a cheerful language, now?"
>
> "Yes," replied Nicholas, "I should say it was, certainly."
>
> "It's very much changed since my time, then," said the collector, "very much."
>
> "Was it a dismal one in your time?" asked Nicholas, scarcely able to repress a smile.
>
> "Very," replied Mr. Lillyvick, with some vehemence of manner. "It's the war time that I speak of; the last war. It may be a cheerful language. I should be sorry to contradict anybody; but I can only say that I've heard the French prisoners, who were natives, and ought to know how to speak it, talking in such a dismal manner, that it made one miserable to hear them. Ay, that I have, fifty times, sir—fifty times!"
>
> [*NN*, chap. 16, pp. 203–04]

One notable thing about the presentation of this proto-Whorfian discussion is that the verbs used in the tags do not draw attention to suprasegmentals. The alternatives to *said* are *asked* and *replied*, the one used twice, the other three times. Neither word supplies information we would not easily gather from the speech to which it is fastened.[48] About the various manner-in-which phrases Dickens includes in his suspensions opinions will differ; and clearly the phrases differ from one another in their informativeness: "with some vehemence of manner" is not needed; "assuming the air of a profound critic" helps a bit. No doubt the entire scene *could* be written without tags, and with no or minor changes in the speeches themselves be just as amusing as it is now. But I do think we misunderstand the psychology of Dickensian authorship, misunderstand also the relationship Dickens establishes with his audience in these early novels, if we assume that Dickens would have eliminated the tags had he only realized they were unnecessary. For his purposes they are *not* unnecessary: he is a divine watchmaker who welcomes, looks for, invents opportunities to come in and oil the works, reset the balances, dust the thing, and wind it.

When he uses a suspended quotation, Dickens interrupts a character long enough to give us a fair reminder of his own scornful, charming, or compassionate self; with the minimal tag—the *said he* or *she replied* Scott or Austen or Gaskell might well omit—Dickens is merely reminding us that he *is* still present. There is a third Dickensian ploy which sometimes is more like the suspended quotation in its effect, sometimes more like the minimal tag. This ploy (noticed by Monod)[49] is the use of what I shall call the booster-shot identification: the interruption of a character's single long speech for the insertion of a second, third, and perhaps fourth speech tag: overt program identification which is covert station identification.

Think back to what was said earlier about the special attractiveness of dialogue and you will see that, other things being equal, a single long speech by a character is not quite as threatening to a narrator as the exchange of short speeches in a duologue: the longer a character goes on speaking, the longer just his one voice is heard, the smaller that character's special advantage over the narrator. Eventually, the long monologue in a novel comes to seem no more attractive than the narrator's descriptive passages. (I suspect that most readers of novels containing such long inset speeches are liminally aware of a sort of click-off point: a moment in which the novelty of the speaker's voice disappears, and that voice becomes ground rather than figure. When this point is reached, we find ourselves looking forward to the end of the speech.) Be that as it may, early Dickens, that splendid egotist, is most reluctant to let either a set of characters or a single character talk on for a while without some reassertion of the bind between author and reader: thus suspended quotations, "uninformative" minimal tags, and also booster-shot identifications.

To sensitize ourselves to the effects of that third device, let us look first at two contrasting examples from the period. These come from Disraeli's *Sybil*, a work without the Dickensian enthusiasm for booster-shots. First, some expert political advice. A character named Mr. Hoaxem—we are, you will notice, at a moment of satire, and that none of the subtlest—asks "the gentleman in Downing Street" how to deal with a delegation of manufacturers:

> "You must say exactly the reverse," said the gentleman in Downing Street. "Show them how much I have done to promote the revival of trade. First of all, in making provisions cheaper; cutting off at one blow half the protection on corn, as, for example, at this moment under the old law the duty on foreign wheat would have been twenty-seven shillings a quarter; under the new law it is thirteen. To be sure no wheat could come in at either price, but that does not alter the principle. Then, as to live cattle, show how I have entirely opened the trade with the Continent in live cattle. Enlarge upon this, the subject is speculative and admits of expensive estimates. If there be any dissenters on the deputation, who, having freed the negroes, have no subject left for their foreign sympathies, hint at the tortures of the bull-fight and the immense consideration to humanity, that, instead of being speared at Seville, the Andalusian Toro will probably in future be cut up at Smithfield. This cheapness of provision will permit them to compete with the foreigner in all neutral markets, in time beat them in

their own. It is a complete compensation too for the property-tax, which, impress upon them, is a great experiment and entirely for their interests. Ring the changes on great measures and great experiments till it is time to go down and make a House. Your official duties, of course, must not be interfered with. They will take the hint. I have no doubt you will get through the business very well, Mr. Hoaxem, particularly if you be 'frank and explicit;' that is the right line to take when you wish to conceal your own mind and to confuse the minds of others. Good morning!"

And with that "Good morning!" Disraeli ends not only the speech but a chapter (VI, 1). The reader of Dickens feels something alien here—or perhaps one should say, an alien tolerance of the alien: surely Dickens would not allow a character to stay in control for this long while making a case for evil practices; in fact, Dickens will not often allow a speaker to amuse us uninterruptedly for this long *whatever* the moral worth of that character or his message. The second speech from Disraeli will sensitize us even more. For here the speaker is not a prime minister but a rather Dickensian type: the tyrannizing son of a tyrant father (rather like the younger Squeers in *Nicholas Nickleby*) and that son (Master Joseph Diggs) is dispensing goods at a company store where all the abuses that go with company stores are to be found. Joseph's speech is, in fact, lightly stylized according to the same convention Mayhew observes in *London Labour and the London Poor;* that is, we are given a monologue, but at certain points it is clear that some interlocutor has said or asked something to which the monologist responds.[50] In spite of this light stylization and in spite of the fact that the character talking does seem imitation Dickens, this speech is painful to read in a way comparable true Dickensian speeches of the period are not. It is the length of the quotation that makes the experience an uncomfortable one; not the absolute length, the number of words, but the sense of a series of outrageous words without a gesture from the author:

"You never want best tea; you must take three ounces of

best tea, or you shan't have nothing. If you say another word, I'll put you down for four. You tall gal, what's your name, you keep back there, or I'll fetch you such a cut as 'll keep you at home till next reckoning. Cuss you, you old fool, do you think I am to be kept all day while you are mumbling here? Who's pushing on there? I see you, Mrs. Page. Won't there be a black mark against you! Oh! it's Mrs. Prance, is it? Father, put down Mrs. Prance for a peck of flour. I'll have order here. You think the last bacon a little too fat: oh! you do, ma'am, do you? I'll take care you shan't complain in futur; I likes to please my customers. There's a very nice flitch hanging up in the engine-room; the men wanted some rust for the machinery; you shall have a slice of that; and we'll say tenpence a pound, high-dried, and wery lean—will that satisfy you?

"Order, there, order; you cussed women, order, or I'll be among you. And if I do jump over this here counter, won't I fly right and left? Speak out, you idiot! do you think I can hear your muttering in this babel? Cuss them; I'll keep them quiet," and so he took up a yard measure, and, leaning over the counter, hit right and left.

[III, chap. 3, pp. 161–62]

And yet God has not said a word. Compare this passage from *Nicholas Nickleby:*

"I think there must be something in the place," *said Mrs. Nickleby, who had been listening in silence;* "for, soon after I was married, I sent to Stratford with my poor dear Mr. Nickleby, in a post-chaise from Birmingham—was it a post-chaise though!" *said Mrs. Nickleby, considering;* "yes, it must have been a post-chaise, because I recollect remarking at the time that the driver had a green shade over his left eye;—in a post-chaise from Birmingham, and after we had seen Shakespeare's tomb and birthplace, we went back to the inn there, where we slept that night, and I recollect that all night long I dreamt of nothing but a black gentleman, at full length, in plaster-of-Paris, with a lay-down collar tied with two tassels, leaning against a post and thinking; and when I woke in the morning and described him to Mr. Nickleby, he said it was Shakespeare just as he had been when he was alive, which was very curious indeed. Stratford—Stratford," *continued Mrs. Nickleby, considering.* "Yes, I am positive about that, because I recollect I was in the family way with my son Nicholas at the time, and I had been very much frightened by an Italian image boy that very morning. In fact, it was quite a mercy, ma'am," *added Mrs. Nickleby, in a whisper to Mrs. Wititterly*, "that my son didn't turn out to be a Shakespeare, and what a dreadful thing that would have been!"

[*Nicholas Nickleby*, chap. 27, p. 353. Italics added]

Or this from *Dombey and Son:*

"Upon my word and honour," *said Mr. Toots, earnestly*, I should be very much obliged to you if you'd improve my acquaintance. I should like to know you, Captain, very much. I really am in want of a friend, I am. Little Dombey was my friend at old Blimber's, and would have been now, if he'd have lived. The Chicken," *said Mr. Toots, in a forlorn whisper*, "is very well—admirable in his way—the sharpest man perhaps in the world; there's not a move he isn't up to, everybody says so—but I don't know—he's not everything. So she *is* an angel, Captain. If there is an angel anywhere, it's Miss Dombey. That's what I've always said. Really though, you know," *said Mr. Toots*, "I should be very much obliged to you if you'd cultivate my acquaintance."

[chap. 32, p. 460. Italics added]

And, for the treatment we expect tyrants to receive in early Dickens, look at two speeches (neither all that long) by Ralph Nickleby:

"I say," *repeated Ralph, tartly*, "let him get that situation, and his fortune is made. If he don't like that, let him get one for himself. Without friends, money, recommendation, or knowledge of business of any kind, let him find honest employment in London which will keep him in shoe leather, and I'll give him a thousand pounds. At least," *said Mr.*

*Ralph Nickleby, checking himself,* "I would if I had it."
[chap. 3, p. 27. Italics added]

Truth to tell, the reader does not need that "checking himself"; but it does our hearts good to hear that sarcastic use of the speaker's full name, Mr. Ralph Nickleby; it is satisfying to be reminded that between us and Ralph there stands someone who is as indignant as we, vigilant, and strong to interrupt.

The second Ralph Nickleby passage is like a moment in a boxing match. For an instant Ralph is unsure of himself, unsteady, his usually efficient speech wanders, and Dickens takes advantage of the unwonted hesitancy to weigh in with a series of jabs:

> "It would be my duty, if he came in my way, to deliver him up to justice," *said Ralph,* "my bounden duty; I should have no other course, as a man of the world and a man of business, to pursue. And yet," *said Ralph, speaking in a very marked manner, and looking furtively, but fixedly, at Kate,* "and yet I would not. I would spare the feelings of his—of his sister. And his mother of course," *added Ralph, as though by an afterthought, and with far less emphasis.*
> [chap. 20, pp. 249–50. Italics added][51]

Like the lengthy suspension, the booster-shot identification is essentially aggressive, and Dickens uses it, whenever possible, in situations where authorial aggressiveness is morally sanctioned or at least inoffensive: with villainous characters or at least comic butts. But even a sympathetic character provokes jealousy when he holds the microphone for a while, and Sam Weller's memorable story of the sausage factory [*Pickwick Papers,* chap. 31, pp. 423–24] will not quite be allowed to reach its end without the rather undistinguished insertion, "said Mr. Weller, looking steadily into Mr. Pickwick's horror-stricken countenance." When a just God is not needed, we find the anxious cicerone: "Yes, Sam's story *is* funny; but look, signore, I make it even funnier. Aren't you glad I'm here?"

The good cicerone wants to show his patrons that he is

attentive and constantly thinking of their needs and desires. He also wants them to find him indispensable. Thus, if he knows his business, he will tell us all about this church just *before* we come to the plaque which explains about this church; he will flick away something from our shoulder before we are quite sure there is anything there to be flicked away. Literally, as narrator, he explains about the tone of some remark so soon that we don't bother asking whether the bare words of that remark would not perfectly well suggest the tone used. And if he is really shrewd, this cicerone, if he suspects we may be thinking we really *do* understand the natives pretty well and that there really *are* quite a number of plaques around, if he has suspicions of this kind and is agile and inventive—he will arrange a few minor accidents. Tact is important here: we must not be allowed to think our guide has become inattentive . . . but if somehow it happens that we should get off into the wrong street or find that listening to the shopkeepers is not quite the same as working with our tutors, and if, happily, our cicerone catches up with us then and makes it all right again . . . that is not a bad thing to have happened; from the cicerone's point of view, an occasional accident of this kind is not at all a bad thing.

The device of the happy accident is, in Dickensian fiction, the belated explanation, the ex post facto explanation. Does the reader think his guide might be a little less solicitous, might leave him alone with the people of the town for a bit longer, in the way the admirable Signor Scott or Signorina Austen does? Well, we will have a demonstration every once in a while of what happens when our cicerone is for some reason unable to keep up, and we are left alone with the townsfolk. There will be confusion; a laughable confusion, and a laughable confusion in which the butt of the laughter will be, in retrospect, the rapidly speaking natives and not our estimable selves . . . but you do see how much I am needed, do you not, *caro lettore?*

Consider this passage from *Dombey and Son:*

"I must entreat," said Mr. Carker, stepping forward, "I

must beg, I must demand, to be released. Slight and unimportant as this difference is—"

Mrs. Skewton, who had been intent upon her daughter's face, took him up here.

"My sweetest Edith," she said, "and my dearest Dombey; our excellent friend Mr. Carker, for so I am sure I ought to mention him—"

Mr. Carker murmured, "Too much honour."

"—has used the very words that were in my mind, and that I have been dying, these ages, for an opportunity of introducing. Slight and unimportant! My sweetest Edith, and my dearest Dombey, do we not know that any difference between you two—No, Flowers, not now."

Flowers was the maid who, finding gentlemen present, retreated with precipitation.

[chap. 36, p. 519]

It is Mrs. Skewton who finally looks ridiculous because of that abrupt shift of subject in her last speech. And yet it is *we* who were confused, who needed to be told who Flowers was. Not a bad lesson for us—especially since this is a scene where, despite the presence of four characters in the room even before the entrance of Flowers, all the authorial comments have been in the dubious-necessity range: five hundred pages into a Dickens novel we might well be able to identify all four speakers by ourselves; might get along with fewer attentions from the narrator.

Flowers fades fast in the memory; few readers will remember their bewilderment even an hour after they have read this passage, where the belated explanation is relatively inconspicuous, a small piece of negative reinforcement. But elsewhere—particularly in the early novels—Dickens uses the device more spectacularly. A good many Dickensians will recall this moment in *Oliver Twist:*

"Drat that beadle!" said Mrs. Mann, hearing the well-known shaking at the garden gate. "If it isn't him at this time in the morning! Lauk, Mr. Bumble, only think of its being you! Well, dear me, it *is* a pleasure, this is! Come into the parlour, sir, please!"

The first sentence was addressed to Susan; and the exclamations of delight were uttered to Mr. Bumble: as the good lady unlocked the garden-gate, and showed him, with great attention and respect, into the house.

[chap. 17, p. 119]

Mrs. Mann is the victim here and deservedly so: it is her hypocrisy which is syncopated by the bewildering form of quotation. True: but the bewilderment, which once more ends in laughter, is not Mrs. Mann's but our own: for a moment we've been left unattended, and we have lost our way.

Still more memorable (and earlier still) is the talk of Mr. Dowler, a new and rather fierce acquaintance of the Pickwickians who explains to them, as they sit waiting for a coach, how he had sent a note which persuaded a rival for his wife's hand to withdraw from the competition:

"I said I had pledged my word as a gentleman to skin him. My character was at stake. I had no alternative. As an officer in His Majesty's service, I was bound to skin him. I regretted the necessity, but it must be done. He was open to conviction. He saw that the rules of the service were imperative. He fled. I married her. Here's the coach. That's her head."

As Mr. Dowler concluded, he pointed to a stage which had just driven up, from the open window of which a rather pretty face in a bright blue bonnet was looking among the crowd on the pavement: most probably for the rash man himself.

[*PP*, chap. 35, p. 493]

And finally we may cite, from *Nicholas Nickleby*, a speech which might have appeared in an avant-garde magazine of the 1920s if it were only cut free from the cicerone paragraph which follows it.

"Yes," said Mr. Folair, with undisturbed calmness, "that's what they say. I thought I'd tell you, because really you ought to know. Oh! here's this blessed phenomenon at last.

> Ugh, you little imposition, I should like to—quite ready, my darling—humbug—Ring up, Mrs. G., and let the favourite wake 'em!"
>
> Uttering in a loud voice such of the latter allusions as were complimentary to the unconscious phenomenon, and giving the rest in a confidential 'aside' to Nicholas, Mr. Folair followed the ascent of the curtain with his eyes. . . .
>
> [chap. 30, p. 387]

Again our bewilderment ends in laughter; and what we come to recognize after a while is that the form of laughter here is genuinely infantile. The laughter inspired by the belated explanation has something in it of the baby's laughter as its mother plays peekaboo, pretends to disappear and then suddenly reappears; the game here is a game of neglect and abandonment, made possible by the greatest confidence that we will never *really* be abandoned, are deeply, even fiercely, loved.[52]

What I have been pursuing through this chapter has been, viewed in one way, a speculative study of the psychology of Dickensian authorship and particularly of Dickens's relation to his readers and his characters. On his relation to his readers, one of the best short statements I know is Monroe Engel's: "Dickens was peculiarly fitted, by disposition and attitude as well as by ambition, to be a popular writer. For one thing, in part because success came to him so quickly, he had no feelings of natural antagonism toward his audience."[53] Certainly this is true; but yet for a man with Dickens's will to power and egocentricity there are possibilities for resentment and antagonism even when immense success comes to him in his early twenties: he may feel slighted if the sales and compliments of the moment do not match those of last year or last month; can wish to be adored in a somewhat different way. He may see it as his responsibility, his job, to earn and keep the public's attention and at the same time conceive of that satisfying of the audience as a controlling of the audience, an exercise in power. (In this connection it is of the greatest interest that, as H. P. Sucksmith has observed, Dickens's comments on the craft of fiction are predominantly affective. Dickens is always telling other writers how to avoid undesirable audience responses and how to make the audience react to something in a work as the author would wish them to.[54] How to control the audience, we may say.) There is all the difference in the world between Dickens noticing that the sales of *Martin Chuzzlewit* are down and a Joyce suffering because of philistinism and readerly incomprehension. But Dickens could not know about Joyce, and the iconography of Chatterton in his garret never meant much to Dickens: a drop in sales was a cause for concern and surely also a humiliation and cause for resentment. And again—beyond these things there is the subtler, less namable potential for authorial resentment and jealousy we have been discussing here.[55]

It is absorbing enough to think about the divisions within an author's psyche and to use stylistic traits as a clue to those divisions. As I have indicated, though, my final interest here is not with the psychology of writing but with the psychology of reading. The heart of the matter, as far as I am concerned, is that the Dickens reader feels that competition within the novels, feels that behind and in these pages is an author who never lets up but is courting and wooing his audience anew in almost every paragraph. No novelist makes us feel as desired as does Dickens.[56]

# *Dickens the Dark, Dickens the Cold*

Oh, for an ancient book of instructions! How nice it would be to have found a Victorian vademecum, a *Whole Art and Symbolism of Writing Conversations*. Discover the right work of this kind, establish the possibility that your writer knew it, and you can go on for pages without using a subjunctive. Historically sanctioned interpretations of rhetorical devices, or iconographic or numerological patterns, allow one to proclaim that readers of intervening generations have been quite wrong about the meaning of a particular work. This, this, just this, is what that reference or trope or triple tercet meant. Well, we are critics of another sort. Obviously the kind of stylistic analysis practiced in the present book makes no claims to the recovery of any system of esoteric signification. Here and there I have pointed out something that would have been more apparent to one of Dickens's first readers than it is to us, but on the whole this study has not been trying to recover something lost: rather, I have been attempting to arrive at a clearer and in some ways richer understanding of what a particular device or work or body of works has meant to its readers all along. Here it cannot be asserted that past readers misunderstood (or present readers misunderstand) a work because they missed some stylistic pattern and its import: one can say only that a reader will be tempted to dismiss certain reactions as extraneous or idiosyncratic or irrelevant until stylistic analysis (even vademecum-less stylistic analysis) legitimates those reactions by showing that they are at least reactions to something intrinsic to the text. And when his reactions seem legitimate (and when, perhaps as important, he discovers that they are shared, at least in part, by others!) that reader is willing to think more carefully about those reactions; and when he thinks more carefully about them, he deepens those reactions.

In any case, our present study has taken us, by a new and winding road, to one of the best-known phenomena of nineteenth-century literary culture: the peculiar closeness of Dickens and his audience. We have seen (and this is a thing at least relatively new) that that closeness of relationship is something built into the novels rather than surrounding them; it is built in not only negatively (one knows that Dickens will not turn on the reader, put him to a test of righteousness, intelligence, or alertness which the reader might fail) but positively: the person telling us about these characters loves us with a jealous love; the jealousy is for us a comfortable and flattering thing, manifested as aggression against rivals rather than snappishness toward the courted. This powerful and charming person seems to need us, to need us far too much to risk offending, to need us far too much even to think of testing. He must hold on, and he makes us feel his need to hold on. The erotic triangle here, the peculiarly intense and intensely peculiar triangle of characters/readers/author, is one of the things which make Charles Dickens World Literature while more responsible and intelligent novelists (George Eliot, for instance) remain English literature. There is nothing quite like that triangular relationship elsewhere—or, more properly, there may be less passionate varieties of it elsewhere in early Victorian fiction (the period liking for suspended quotations would lead us to suspect this) but nowhere else does this relationship have its

Dickensian intensity. In this respect Dickens may be hyper-Victorian and thus a new thing under the sun.

Now one might reasonably stop here, be content with a new understanding of the way in which Dickens meant (and, for a nonacademic audience, pretty much still means) what he did in the nineteenth century. But there is another use to which we may put the ideas about Dickensian style we have been developing.

The best-known fact in the history of Dickens criticism is of course the reaction of the new Dickensians against the old; the tendency of highly educated twentieth-century readers to see Dickens as an artist whose vision darkened and matured as he grew older and whose later works are far greater than his earlier, more popular ones: greater in social and psychological insight, greater in artistic design. Now I think I ought to confess here that in so far as I take sides in this quarrel my sympathies are with the Micawberian loyalists: I simply think *David Copperfield* modifies human consciousness uniquely while *Little Dorrit* is an honorable *et cetera* work, a good novel of local importance. This, however, is a preference I confess rather than argue for. What does concern me here is to show that the stylistic habits we have been discussing may help us to understand the distaste the old Dickensians felt for many or all of Dickens's later novels; may help us to understand what was new in the new Dickens, the dark Dickens.

Those readers who objected to the late Dickens—at least the objectors who interest me—find something cold, mechanical, in those post-*Copperfield* novels. Thus, two paragraphs from Henry James's review of *Our Mutual Friend:*

> *Our Mutual Friend* is, to our perception, the poorest of Mr. Dickens's works. And it is poor with the poverty not of momentary embarrassment, but of permanent exhaustion. It is wanting in inspiration. For the last ten years it has seemed to us that Mr. Dickens has been unmistakeably forcing himself. *Bleak House* was forced; *Little Dorrit* was laboured; the present work is dug out as with a spade and pickaxe. . . .

> To say that the conduct of the story, with all its complications, betrays a long-practised hand, is to pay no compliment worthy the author. If this were, indeed, a compliment, we should be inclined to carry it further, and congratulate him on his success in what we should call the manufacture of fiction; for in so doing we should express a feeling that has attended us throughout the book. Seldom, we reflected, had we read a book so intensely *written*, so little seen, known, or felt.[1]

Stephen Leacock, a warmer admirer of the early Dickens than was James, speaks of the "overplanned and uninspired work of much of the later books."[2] Overplanned . . . forced—I want to suggest that readers who made such complaints need not have been either insensitive to the value of design in fiction or incapable of enjoying works without comic characters of the Weller-Micawber-Gamp varieties. (Certainly neither charge could be made against James!) The new Dickensians can make the old Dickensians look foolish because whenever the old Dickensians try to analyze precisely what it is that goes wrong in the post-*Copperfield* novels, try to account for their sense that something is missing, they sound (or can be made to sound) silly and sentimental, escapists or philistines. (Only Chesterton, who relies on metaphor and paradox more than analysis, escapes humiliation.) But there *was* something those old Dickensians were on to, there was a change they perceived which was not simply a function of changing social vision or changing ideas about the organization of a novel. And I think we can use some of our earlier findings to get *at* the things that got *to* the old Dickensians. One would hardly say that some change in the presentation of dialogue is *the* difference between early and late Dickens. I do claim that things of this kind, minor changes, "inconspicuous" ones, are more important than we think. The old Dickensians felt that in his later works their novelist had lost his touch or possessed it only intermittently, uncertainly. What I want to suggest is that we understand both those old Dickensians and Dickens himself more profitably if we approach this loss of touch not simply as a failure to provide jolly characters but as a loss of phatic communion: a drawing away from the old triangular relationship or, better, a lessening of the intensity of that relationship.

I shall try to get at some of the stylistic causes for this change in Dickens's relations with his readers in two ways. First, I will do some more or less traditional explicating and present a close reading of one well-known chapter in late Dickens and brief discussions of a few other characteristic passages. Then, as a sort of supplement to those local explications, I will present some numerical data. The latter, my excursion into statistics, is intended to be no more than supplementary and suggestive. In any case, I should begin by pointing out one theme common to both my local explications and supplementary counts. The stylistic pattern of late Dickens is one that a nineteenth-century reader would naturally have seen against two different grounds: the ground of "period style," of whatever appears the usual thing for novelists to do, and the ground of early Dickens.[3] As far as habits of quotation are concerned, late Dickens seen against the one ground is subtly different from late Dickens seen against the other. The subtlety of this difference is one of the things that have made the changes we are trying to point out so difficult to point out: the changes in the author's attitude toward his readers.

First, then, the practical criticism and a demonstration of what it means to read late Dickens against our memories of early Dickens, of how the background of early Dickens really affects our understanding of the later novels. For this exercise in explication I select the initial chapter of *Hard Times*—first, because *Hard Times* is notoriously the Dickens novel least liked by the older Dickensians, and second, because we have available an interesting and well-known reading of this chapter by David Lodge—a reading which makes no *use* of early Dickens. Let me remind you of what Lodge says about that opening and then present my second, alternative reading.

After a discussion of the wildly differing opinions about

the esthetic value of *Hard Times*, Lodge proceeds to give a careful analysis of various linguistic patterns in the novel's first paragraphs. He concludes:

> The technique of the first chapter of *Hard Times* could not be described as "subtle." But subtle effects are often lost in a first chapter, where the reader is coping with the problem of "learning the author's language." Perhaps with some awareness of this fact, sharpened by his sense of addressing a vast, popular audience, Dickens begins many of his novels by nailing the reader's attention with a display of sheer rhetorical power, relying particularly on elaborate repetition. One thinks, for instance, of the fog at the beginning of *Bleak House* or the sun and shadow in the first chapter of *Little Dorrit*. In these novels the rhetoric works hard to establish a symbolic atmosphere; in *Hard Times*, to establish a thematic Idea—the despotism of Fact. But this abstraction—Fact—is invested with a remarkable solidity through the figurative dimension of the language.
>
> The gross effect of the chapter is simply stated, but analysis reveals that it is achieved by means of a complex verbal activity which is far from simple. Whether it represents fairly any actual educational theory or practice in mid-nineteenth-century England is really beside the point. It aims to convince us of the *possibility* of children being taught in such a way, and to make us recoil from the imagined possibility. The chapter succeeds or fails as rhetoric; and I think it succeeds.[4]

Here I would argue that that "vast, popular audience" was there for chapter 1 precisely because it thought it already *knew* the author's language. What it is learning is that the author's language has changed, and the change in the language is itself a message. Attached to the thematic idea of the despotism of Fact we find: reader, I care more about my hatred for this thing than I care about your love; don't get in the way of my hatred.

Let us look, paragraph by paragraph, at that first short

chapter. Here is the famous opening speech: seventy-seven words about facts:

> "Now, what I want is, Facts. Teach these boys and girls nothing but Facts. Facts alone are wanted in life. Plant nothing else, and root out everything else. You can only form the minds of reasoning animals upon Facts: nothing else will ever be of any service to them. This is the principle on which I bring up my own children, and this is the principle on which I bring up these children. Stick to Facts, Sir!"

This is the *Sentimental Journey* ploy, the opening with dialogue; but here there is no sense of play or innuendo ("They order," said I, "this matter better in France") nor is there any suggestion of an *interesting* mystery: "Now, what I want is, Facts" is not at all the same kind of thing as "Certainly, when I threw her from the garret window to the stony pavement below, I did not anticipate that she would fall so far without injury to life or limb." If we are experienced readers of early Dickens coming upon that *Hard Times* paragraph for the first time, we know the speaker of these words is not going to be a likable character; in Dickens likable characters do not use expressions like "form the minds of reasoning animals" when discussing children. No *enticing* secret behind this opening paragraph, no authorial teasing of the reader, no courting of the reader; we are simply thrust into the company of someone who is repulsive in no very amusing way—this is no Quilp or Bumble—and at the same time thrust into a situation which is obscure without being mysterious. We do stay around—we are not going to give up on the new Dickens novel this early—and thus we must play the game and ask the questions raised by the passage's uninviting obscurity. Who is the speaker? Who is addressed? Where? Who *are* these boys and girls? But in fact—if you will pardon the expression—we may notice that something very odd happens when we play the game and allow these questions to form in our minds. We are, as I have said, pretty sure this speaker is a bad 'un. We know what this character likes is Facts. But those questions we are asking ourselves, are *they* not questions about Facts: who? to whom? where? Not only is our officious cicerone unwontedly slack in his attentions, but our bewilderment, our dawning sense of a breach of Dickensian contract, is associating us with an unsympathetic character. (It seems to me, by the bye, that the uncomfortableness of this opening—the reader in need of facts listening to an unattractive character stress the importance of facts—probably is felt even by readers who do not know the earlier Dickens novels: but of course the stronger our sense of forties Dickens as a norm, the stronger our sense of dislocation and sourness here.)

Now the second paragraph, which is narrative rather than quotation, helps us: but perhaps less than we might have expected:

> The scene was a plain, bare, monotonous vault of a schoolroom, and the speaker's square forefinger *emphasized* his observations by underscoring every sentence with a line on the schoolmaster's sleeve. *The emphasis was helped by* the speaker's square wall of a forehead, which had his eyebrows for its base, while his eyes found commodious cellerage in two dark caves, overshadowed by the wall. *The emphasis was helped* by the speaker's mouth, which was wide, thin, and hard set. *The emphasis was helped by* the speaker's voice, which was inflexible, dry, and dictatorial. *The emphasis was helped by* the speaker's hair, which bristled on the skirts of his bald head, a plantation of firs to keep the wind from its shining surface, all covered with knobs, like the crust of a plum pie, as if the head had scarcely warehouse-room for the hard facts stored inside. The speaker's obstinate carriage, square coat, square legs, square shoulders—nay, his very neckcloth, trained to take him by the throat with an unaccommodating grasp, like a stubborn fact, as it was,—*all helped the emphasis.*

[Italics added]

Certain questions of fact are answered: this is a schoolroom, and in addition to the speaker there is a schoolmaster present, who is presumably the "you" addressed in the preceding paragraph. If we want to look at the paragraph *very* closely, though, we may say that *presumably* there is a schoolmaster present. What we *know* is that a schoolmaster's sleeve is present—which is to say that even here, in the second paragraph, our cicerone is not at pains to answer the questions which his patrons wish to have answered: we must infer the answer to the question Who is this *you*? from something said almost in passing about the way the (still unidentified) speaker emphasizes the points he makes. And this fact in turn brings our attention to something curious about the sequence of paragraphs: while the second of them does provide meager answers to some of the questions which occurred to us as we read through the first, it is only the first clause of this new paragraph ("The scene was a plain, bare, monotonous vault of a schoolroom . . .") which is directly concerned with one of those questions. The rest of the paragraph is really about suprasegmentals: thus, instead of our first narrative paragraph telling us all that we wanted to know, answering the questions that occurred to us about the context of what the speaker said, its main thrust is to make us reimagine the speech itself, virtually to read it again.[5] The fact that the second paragraph *is* a new paragraph and that it begins with a clause about the setting is subtly misleading: we thought we were done with the speaker's act of communication *as* act of communication; but we were wrong. The five uses of *helped* are ironic in more than one way: this character, more and more evidently someone not to be liked, is emphasizing *facts*, and every repulsive or absurd thing about him *helps* the emphasis. Our Dickensian cicerone is not helping us, his fact-starved patrons. The plum pie simile (to which Lodge sternly objects) sounds like our old charming guide: but then again, that guide was not only satirical at the expense of the characters but anxious to endear himself to us: it is far from clear that *both* things are still true.

The chapter ends:

"In this life, we want nothing but Facts, Sir; nothing but Facts!"

The speaker, and the schoolmaster, and the third grown person present, all backed a little, and swept with their eyes the inclined plane of little vessels then and there arranged in order, ready to have imperial gallons of facts poured into them until they were full to the brim.

Much as we began the second paragraph of *Hard Times* assuming we were done with the speech as speech and found we were wrong, we discover from the third paragraph that the speech is still not over. This third paragraph is of course very short, and so it comes as no surprise to us that it is pure dialogue: we may wonder, though, why this sentence does come as a separate paragraph, since it contains the words of the speaker already quoted and thus might easily have come at the end of the first or second paragraph. We may also notice that here there is no tag (for example, "added the speaker," "concluded the gentleman") to give us the sort of help the earlier Dickens frequently gave us. But far more important, I think, is what happens in that fourth and last paragraph. Yes, it is now quite certain that the schoolmaster is present and not just his sleeve; "these boys and girls" are there in the room ("little vessels" will give us no serious trouble). But the speaker remains unnamed and unidentified, and we're told, virtually in passing, that there is a *third* adult present: a new trouble, this, a new demand that we significantly change our idea of what we've seen. No hint here that the narrator is trying to create suspense, has been holding back information in a significant or amusing way: he is simply not solicitous of our comfort, is not the Dickens of old. Where a device like the catchword quotation seemed to make the character halt in his speech and resume only when the audience's intellectual comfort had been seen to, here—in part because of the substantial initial quotation, in part because of the paratactic effect of the three-paragraph speech/narration/speech presentation—we have the sense that *we* are the ones who have to start the speech over again; and this when the speaker being spared authorial interruptions is evidently someone Dickens despises and where the information withheld from us is not kept back in order to increase our enjoyment at some later moment of revelation.

Chesterton writes of *Hard Times*, "Twenty times we have taken Dickens's hand and it has been sometimes hot with revelry and sometimes weak with weariness; but this time we start a little, for it is inhumanly cold; and then we realise we have touched his gauntlet of steel."[6] Yes. The question we want to consider is not simply one of the darkness of such a work as *Hard Times* but the coldness of such a work: the experience of the old Dickensian is more tactile than visual. And yes, the "start" comes from the contrast between what we feel now and what we felt in the past. Only "inhumanly" is wrong: it is simply an un-Dickensian coldness; it is not that we cannot bear this climate, it is that we did not expect this climate in this area. The most deeply disturbing thing is not the new vision of the world as a muddle or too deeply troubled to be set right by the "philosophie de noël"; it is his distance from the reader, his leaving of the phatic gesture, the finger upon the sleeve, for the Gradgrinds.

The opening chapter of *Hard Times* is of course the portrait of a character Dickens dislikes; the paucity of humor in the book may be seen as an experiment, and the failure of the Sleary group to enthrall us simply as a failure—either ours or the author's. We grant all this, grant also, of course, the large things, the changing social vision, but still feel that there is a difference unaccounted for. It is just here, in a situation of this kind, that the most minute sort of stylistic analysis can be stimulating: for stylistic analysis, though it cannot in itself explain the meaning of a change, can provide evidence that a change is more far-reaching than we had been told it was, that the explanations we have do not explain enough. Let us return now to our particular concern, the presentation of direct discourse. We take up a different sort of scene from *Hard Times*, a pathetic scene. Stephen Blackpool and Rachael sit by the bed of Stephen's wife. The Dickens of the forties would, I think, probably have presented

Rachael's words to Stephen in something like the following way:

> "I came to do what little I could, Stephen," said Rachael. "First, for that she worked with me when we were girls both, and for that you courted her and married her when I was her friend; and next," continued Rachael, as he laid his furrowed forehead on his hand with a low groan, "and next, for that I know your heart, and am right sure and certain that 'tis far too merciful to let her die, or even so much as suffer, for want of aid. Thou knowest," said Rachael, "thou knowest who said, 'Let him who is without sin among you cast the first stone at her!' There have been plenty to do that. Thou art not the man to cast the last stone, Stephen, when she is brought so low."

As it actually appears in *Hard Times*, this is (starting one line earlier):

> He slowly moved to a chair and sat down, drooping his head before her.
>
> "I came to do what little I could, Stephen; first, for that she worked with me when we were girls both, and for that you courted her and married her when I was her friend—"
>
> He laid his furrowed forehead on his hand, with a low groan.
>
> "And next, for that I know your heart, and am right sure and certain that 'tis far too merciful to let her die, or even so much as suffer, for want of aid. Thou knowest who said 'Let him who is without sin among you cast the first stone at her!' There have been plenty to do that. Thou art not the man to cast the last stone, Stephen, when she is brought so low."
>
> [I, chap. 13, p. 83]

This second version—that is to say, the genuine text—does not in itself seem cold to any reader; but it is without the peculiar warmth of Dickens in the forties. Here paragraphing and punctuation take the place of verbal connections: the paragraph-paratactic style. The author disappears, and the *inquit, ergo sum* impulse to mix his words with those of the characters is apparently not felt at this moment. We read this passage and are unaware of the presence or attitudes of the person who is writing it; much as in the first chapter, the writer seemed not at all interested in us.

Something like the arrangement of the Rachael-Stephen scene would be a stylistic oddity in *Oliver Twist* or *Nicholas Nickleby*, but such presentations are quite ordinary in the last fifteen years of Dickens's career. The later works contain conversations where the author is no more obtrusive than the narrator in a Jane Austen duologue. In chapter 13 of *A Tale of Two Cities*, for instance:

> "Since it is my misfortune, Mr. Carton, to have made you more unhappy than you were before you knew me——"
>
> "Don't say that, Miss Manette, for you have reclaimed me, if anything could. You will not be the cause of my becoming worse."
>
> "Since the state of your mind that you describe is, at all events, attributable to some influence of mine—this is what I mean, if I can make it plain—can I use no influence to serve you? Have I no power for good, with you, at all?"
>
> "The utmost good that I am capable of now, Miss Manette, I have come here to realise. Let me carry through the rest of my misdirected life, the remembrance that I opened my heart to you, last of all the world; and that there was something left in me at this time which you could deplore and pity."
>
> [I, chap. 13, pp. 144–45]

These are just four out of a run of eleven pathetic speeches in which, *mirabile dictu*, the author of *The Old Curiosity Shop* introduces not a single word of narrative.

Yes, things look somewhat different. But just about now various "buts" and "althoughs" swarm around us unpleasantly. Statements like "this second version . . . does not in itself seem cold to any reader" make one a bit uneasy; the name Jane Austen does not invariably suggest chill remoteness. There are difficulties in what I've been suggesting in these last pages, and underlying those difficulties is that interesting question of the proper ground against which to view late Dickensian style.

Formally the presentation of Lucie's conversation with Sydney in the last passage quoted from *A Tale of Two Cities* is a use of the Jane Austen/Walter Scott technique and thus represents a change from the normative Dickensian manner of the 1840s. But what other fiction is being published and read in the years of *Hard Times* and *A Tale of Two Cities*? Don't such younger contemporaries of Dickens as Anthony Trollope and Wilkie Collins write longish untagged duologues? For that matter, didn't Scott continue to be read as a "modern" by the Victorians? And, to complicate things further, haven't some of our examples of the suspended quotation (including Mrs. Joe's outburst at the forge) come from the later Dickens? It is one thing to say a passage like the first chapter of *Hard Times* in part achieves its effects by departing from earlier Dickensian norms; but does the Sydney Carton-Lucie Manette exchange really suggest authorial detachment? Certainly we are not bewildered there (or in the Stephen-Rachael scene) as we are in the *Hard Times* opening: it seems reasonable to say that the reader of *A Tale of Two Cities*, whatever he has or has not read before, is simply not thinking about the author at this moment and concentrates on the pathos of the speeches themselves. Finally, can't we find at least one example of any stylistic device we have mentioned in any novel by Dickens? Perhaps in any Regency or Victorian novel?

It all seems a muddle, a number of conflicting patterns. Yes; but perhaps a conflict of patterns is, after all, just what one ought to expect. If we think about the author himself, we may rephrase our earlier hypothesis in this way: Charles Dickens, one of the most egocentric Englishmen of the nineteenth century, was subservient to his readers, terribly anxious for their approval, seemingly afraid to lose contact with them; that authorial anxiety, manifested in certain stylistic preferences, helped create the particular closeness readers felt to the author of the early novels. Now surely it would be odd if Dickens did *not* eventually rebel against this one form of subservience which had freed him from all other forms of subservience? Such rebellion would of course be quite as irrational and unjustifiable as it would be predictable. One would, then, expect the rebellion to be indirect, ambiguous, muffled—a sort of extension of the belated explanation technique. One would expect Dickens to hide such an unreasonable sort of rebellion, such ingratitude, from himself. A muddle, a confusion of patterns, is also what we should expect if we think about the old Dickensians' impression of something gone wrong in the later novels, and their difficulty in explaining the badness of the changes they sense. If we accord those readers a certain measure of respect, we should assume that they had difficulty pinning the thing down because the thing was difficult to pin down; we should expect the changes (including the symptomatic stylistic ones we are studying in this book) to be ambiguous, polyvalent, difficult to name.

At this point, as I have indicated, we may do well to supplement our close readings of particular episodes and conversations with a statistical overview. Our area of interest is the presentation of direct discourse. Let us take as "neutral," or unmarked or normative, all brief medial tags (that is, all explicit inquits containing no more than four words) and also all initial or final tags (of whatever length) which explicitly indicate the producer of a quoted speech. What we shall count, then, is the frequency of two practices which, according to the ideas we presented in our second chapter, represent opposite tendencies. First, the use of suspensions (inquits, etc., five words or more in length), which we have come to associate with authorial intrusiveness; second, the use of untagged (and "hint") quotations: withdrawal by the writer, nonnormative inexplicitness.

Now our first interest is in the style of early Dickens compared with that of late Dickens. We'll give figures for each of the novels here, but our primary concern is not with individual novels but rather with what most readers have felt to be two parts of the novelistic *oeuvre:* early Dickens (*Pickwick* to *Copperfield*) and late Dickens (*Bleak House* to *Edwin Drood*). We shall treat each of these groups as a "population" and take a sampling of 4,000 directly quoted speeches to represent each. Those 4,000 will be made up of 100-speech sequences, randomly selected except in that each 100-speech sequence will begin with the first directly quoted speech in some chapter. Since there are eight novels in the early Dickens group and only seven in the late Dickens group, we cannot, of course, have an equal sampling for each of our two populations and also an equal sampling from each of our novels. I don't know that it matters very greatly whether we are untidy about our two samplings or about our samplings per novel. But since I am more interested in the impression created by those two unofficial entities Early Dickens and Late Dickens than by individual novels, and don't want to encourage a false sense of the accuracy of our figures for individual novels, I choose to be neat in sampling the larger populations rather than the smaller ones: thus I will take five 100-speech sequences from each of the eight early novels *(Pickwick Papers, Oliver Twist, Nicholas Nickleby, Old Curiosity Shop, Barnaby Rudge, Martin Chuzzlewit, Dombey and Son, David Copperfield)* and six from each of the seven novels in the late group—except for *Edwin Drood* and *A Tale of Two Cities*, which will be represented by five samplings each. I shall first count untagged quotations and here find an agreeably spectacular difference. The early novels have an average of 7.4 percent of their directly quoted speeches untagged, and the late novels an average of 32.5 percent. We may also notice that none of our 100-speech samples from the early novels comes near that average density of untagged speeches in the late novels: one sampling from *The Old Curiosity Shop* contains 22 untagged speeches, and the next highest reading among the early 100-speech samples is 16. (I have no doubt that there *are* runs of dialogue with at least one-third of the speeches untagged: the point is that runs of this kind are highly unusual there.)

When we turn to suspensions, we find a notable difference between the two groups, though not one as striking as the difference in the tagged/untagged count. My sampling suggests that the early Dickens uses suspensions of five or more words an average of 30.4 times in 100 directly quoted speeches, and the later Dickens 19.4 times in 100 speeches. (Three of the forty runs from late Dickens come close to the average early Dickensian frequency of suspension [30, 29, 27], though no sampling from late Dickens has a greater number of suspensions than the average early Dickens sampling.)

Looking at these figures and at the others in Appendix 2, one is tempted to say that the difference in texture we are discussing—the difference between early and late Dickens—must have more to do, as far as the presentation of dialogue is concerned, with a changed enthusiasm for untagged quotations than it does with a changed enthusiasm for suspensions. One notices, for instance (if one makes use of the figures for individual works), that the transitional novels *David Copperfield* and *Bleak House* do not differ very greatly in their use of suspensions (25.6 percent in *David Copperfield*, 21 percent in *Bleak House*) but more dramatically in percentages of untagged quotations (9 percent in *Copperfield*, 24.7 percent in *Bleak House*); and of course one also notices, as I have said, that the change in the number of suspensions as one moves from the first to the second group is considerably smaller than the change in the number of tagged quotations. These things are true enough, but one does have to recall here the nature of the occurrences being counted. Item for item, the suspended quotation is rather more conspicuous than the untagged quotation. One may wonder: which would strike a nineteenth-century reader as more different: a pair of novels which differed by 10 percent in quotations suspended or a pair of novels which differed by 25 percent in quotations untagged? A difficult question, it seems to me; but also a question we may leave undiscussed. For the point, surely, is that the two changes we are considering—from more to fewer suspended quotations, from fewer to more untagged quotations—both work to lessen the reader's awareness of authorial solicitude: to lower the temperature of the story-telling, one might say. Let us, in fact, consider the two changes together. We can do this easily enough by disregarding our knowledge about the greater dignity and importance of the suspension (our knowledge that it is more conspicuous item for item than the simple tag;

that it is, according to our theory, always aggressive and disruptive, while the tag is not necessarily either) and merely subtracting the number of untagged quotations in a given run from the number of suspensions. The resultant figure we may call the Officiousness Index of that run. This index, it must be confessed, is not the sort of measurement a statistician would take seriously; it is not good science to yoke two different binary counts together in so simple a way. However, my purpose here is not to prove mathematically but to suggest and stimulate; and to this end the index is almost melodramatically effective. Therefore, I will set out the Officiousness Numbers for Early Dickens, Late Dickens, and also for the samples from each novel (in this table, and the ones that follow, column A gives the average number of suspensions, column B the average number of untagged quotations, and column C the Officiousness Index):

Table 1. Early Dickens

| Work | A | B | C |
|---|---|---|---|
| *Pickwick Papers* | 24.2 | 6.2 | +18.0 |
| *Oliver Twist* | 31.2 | 3.8 | +27.4 |
| *Nicholas Nickleby* | 28.8 | 5.4 | +23.4 |
| *Old Curiosity Shop* | 35.4 | 7.4 | +28.0 |
| *Barnaby Rudge* | 37.2 | 11.6 | +25.6 |
| *Martin Chuzzlewit* | 30.0 | 10.4 | +19.6 |
| *Dombey and Son* | 31.0 | 5.8 | +25.2 |
| *David Copperfield* | 25.6 | 9.0 | +16.6 |

Table 2. Late Dickens

| Work | A | B | C |
|---|---|---|---|
| *Bleak House* | 21.0 | 24.7 | -3.7 |
| *Hard Times* | 20.0 | 26.7 | -6.7 |
| *Little Dorrit* | 21.8 | 31.3 | -9.5 |
| *Tale of Two Cities* | 17.4 | 39.6 | -22.2 |
| *Great Expectations* | 21.3 | 29.0 | -7.7 |
| *Our Mutual Friend* | 19.0 | 33.0 | -14.0 |
| *Edwin Drood* | 13.8 | 46.4 | -32.6 |

Working from our forty 100-speech runs from early Dickens and our forty 100-speech runs from late Dickens we come up with the averages:

| | | | |
|---|---|---|---|
| Early Dickens | 30.4 | 7.4 | +23.0 |
| Late Dickens | 19.4 | 32.45 | -13.1 |

You will notice, of course, that all of the Officiousness Indexes for Early Dickens are positive, all those for Late Dickens negative: in other words, early Dickens characteristically has more suspensions than untagged quotations, late Dickens the reverse. This is an amusing discovery, and allows one to construct a most dramatic graph of Dickens's career:

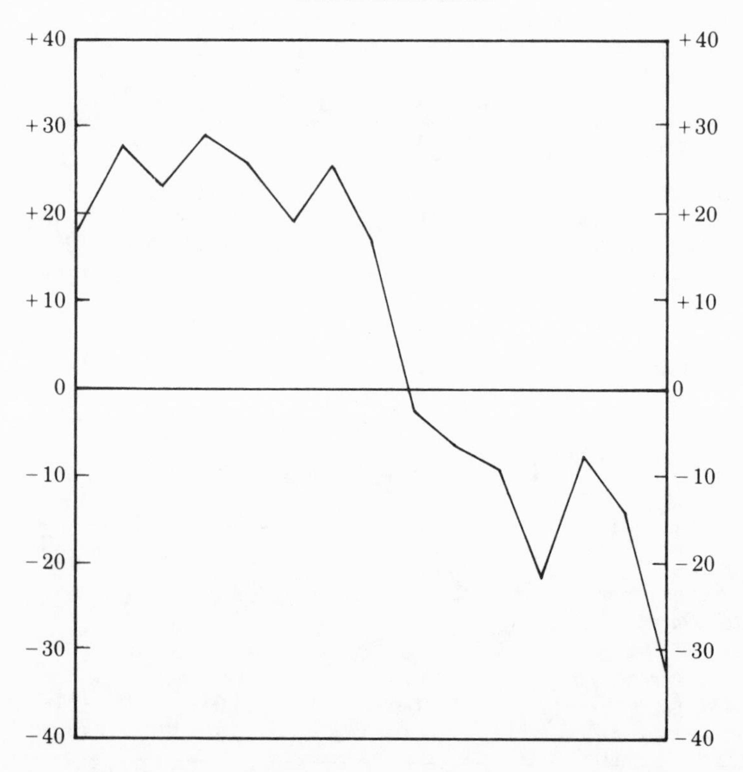

Now of course even the most precise and mathematically elegant counts of linguistic features would not prove anything about readerly reactions to those features, would not prove anything about stylistic effects. On the other hand, even such simple counts as we have here can be valuable to the critic as checks, comforts, or (when the counts don't come out as one thought they should) spurs to further thought. The counts given thus far serve quite well as a modest supplement to modest explications of late Dickens; it is my contention that Dickens grows not simply darker but colder in his late novels, and one would expect to find some manifestations of that increased coldness in his style of quoting. Here it is nice to have the data on Dickensian untagged and suspended quotations.

Now comes the second, procedurally more difficult, part of my task. One would like some statistical indication of how Dickens's practice (or rather his two practices, the early and the late) appeared against some nineteenth-century but non-Dickensian ground. From what novels should the samples be drawn here? How many samples should be taken from each? One could spend a good deal of time discussing such questions, but I think the following commonsense solution will make the results interesting in a commonsense way. To represent a non-Dickensian early nineteenth-century population, I take, once more, a group of forty 100-speech runs. I use the same principles of selection as before but this time, because I do want to include a fair spread of works, I have fewer samplings from each book. (Five or three, depending mostly on the length of the book. *Frankenstein* is represented by only two runs, but those two include virtually all the direct quotations in the novel.) These books, then, were all written between the beginning of the nineteenth century and the end of Dickens's early phase. (Once again, columns A, B, and C are percentage of suspensions, percentage of untagged quotations, and officiousness index. The number after each title is the number of 100-speech runs examined.)

**Table 3. Earlier Nineteenth-Century Novels**

| Work | A | B | C |
|---|---|---|---|
| *Waverley* (5) | 14.0 | 39.8 | -25.8 |
| *Emma* (3) | 8.7 | 41.3 | -32.6 |
| *Frankenstein* (2) | 9.0 | 31.5 | -22.5 |
| *Vanity Fair* (5) | 19.8 | 7.2 | +12.6 |
| *Jane Eyre* (3) | 4.7 | 55.7 | -51.0 |
| *Wuthering Heights* (3) | 16.7 | 10.0 | +6.7 |
| *Mary Barton* (5) | 8.8 | 45.0 | -36.2 |
| *Sybil* (5) | 11.6 | 28.2 | -16.6 |
| *Yeast* (3) | 6.0 | 60.0 | -54.0 |
| *Windsor Castle* (3) | 11.0 | 0.3 | +10.7 |
| *Handley Cross* (3) | 44.0 | 3.7 | +40.3 |
| Averages for the forty runs are: | 14.1 | 29.4 | -15.3 |

They are suggestive, these figures, and I do want to say a word or two about a couple of them. First of all, notice that the novel here which seems more Dickensian than Dickens in its use of suspensions is *Handley Cross*, a relentlessly comic work whose narrator repeatedly interrupts to indicate the grotesqueness of "suprasegmentals" and welcomes the momentary humiliation of speakers in passage after passage. Surtees, in other words, is almost always looking for a chance to do one of the things that radically aggressive device, the suspended quotation, most easily—one might add, most naturally—helps a writer do: make characters seem ridiculous. Surtees employs the device again and again because he wants this one sort of local effect again and again. There is nothing problematic here; one does not feel with Surtees, as one does with Dickens, that the common denominator of the suspensions must be sought below the level of local, immediate effect. About Thackeray, who has the next highest average number of suspensions, a good deal might be said. It is interesting that both he and Surtees are Old Convention novelists; interesting, too, that *Vanity Fair* returns so often to the theme of the characters as puppets. But these ideas are not the important ones for us just now. The point is that even Thackeray's style of quotations is not as warm, "officious," as the style of the early Dickens. Once again it must be stressed that construction of our non-Dickensian context for the early Dickens is rather more art than science. I have taken small samplings from eleven books. A clever scholar could argue for the inclusion of fifty other books; a pedant could argue for the inclusion of another two hundred. And again, one does not want to forget that a good writer controls his style of quotation as least as much as he is controlled by it. We bear all this in mind: but it does nonetheless seem clear that, as a novelist who wanted to do more than just make 'em laugh, make 'em weep, and make 'em wait, the early Dickens had a notably warm style of quotation.

Now it is here, of course, that we come to the double background of Dickens's later quoting style. If a reader had read *only* early Dickens and then plunged into the later novels, he would sense the change, certainly, though he might not be able to name it, and though (again) he would not find every chapter of late Dickens different in quotation style from early Dickens. Still, he would sense a change. But consider late Dickens against the background of those other nineteenth-century novels and he does not seem so cold: to judge by our samplings, even late Dickens has an average use of suspensions which is greater than that of nine of our eleven non-Dickensian novels. His officiousness indexes are now all negative—but so are the indexes for seven out of the eleven novels in the non-Dickensian group. Let us look at a few other Victorian novels coming out while Dickens was publishing his late works:

**Table 4. Five Mid-Victorian Novels**

| Work | A | B | C |
|---|---|---|---|
| *The Virginians* (5) | 13.8 | 19.2 | -5.4 |
| *Adam Bede* (5) | 25.0 | 25.6 | -0.6 |
| *Woman in White* (5) | 7.4 | 43.8 | -36.4 |
| *Can You Forgive Her?* (5) | 9.8 | 51.2 | -41.4 |
| *Alice in Wonderland* (3) | 14.3 | 1.3 | +13.0 |

George Eliot's heavy use of suspensions is striking, especially since one does not think of her as "like" the early Dickens: here, obviously, one might go on to do three different things: first, try some more counting in George Eliot. Second, if the new data look like the data here (and, in fact, I'm pretty sure they will), go on to consider the possibility that yes, George Eliot and Charles Dickens may indeed be particularly like one another in certain respects. Third, one might come up with finer gauge nets, more elaborate categories of suspensions which would make early Dickensian practice distinct from Eliot's later practice. For the moment, though, it will be enough to notice that the heavy proportion of untagged quotations to suspensions distinguishes what Eliot is doing at this time and what Dickens had done earlier. The important thing, just now, is to see how inconspicuously our average figures for late Dickens would fit into this group of five. So would the late Dickens figures fit in well with the figures for the non-Dickensian gang of eleven. In his quotation style, late Dickens looks to be well within the normal range, and warmer than most, when viewed against period usage as that period's usage is reflected in the 6,300 speeches of our non-Dickensian samples. It is only when late Dickens is viewed against the ground of early Dickens that he appears cold. Now you see it, now you don't —better, now you sense it, now you don't, for we must remember that styles in direct quotation were *not* a topic of Victorian discussion, *not* something about which Victorian writers or readers thought it worthwhile to speak. Very hard to put one's finger on: but we have reason to expect that the things in the late Dickens which are not simply laudable "maturity" of one sort or another are going to be, have been, hard to put one's finger on.

What are we saying then about quotation style and the late Dickens? We posit that the old Dickensians were on to something they could not quite name and that it is indeed an essential quality of late Dickens that what is discomforting is also elusive: there is a darkening of vision which may find confirmation in new political attitudes, for instance, but is not fully explained by those attitudes. That elusiveness is well served by the sort of stylistic situation I have described; one would expect to find like stylistic situations in other areas of Dickensian usage: polysyllabic humor, for instance, or double preposition ornateness ("with a view to," "in consequence of," etc.). Late Dickens becomes a figure somewhat like the villain in a Victorian detective story (Sir Percival, say, in *The Woman in White*). Everything is quite *comme il faut*, and yet. . . . There's nothing odd here, this is the way novelists do things . . . but this is not the way *Dickens* does things. Dickens is writing as a proper novelist, helping us according to his bond, no more nor less. It is the sense of a *special* relationship between author and reader which is disrupted, a relationship built up in large part by devices (for example, the ones we have been studying in this book) which we normally do not stop to analyze, and whose withdrawal therefore affects us without our knowing what it is that affects us, what has made things seem colder. And then, even if we should stumble onto one of the right paths, there are so many moments when all seems comfortable again and Dickens is our friendly cicerone still!

For the man Charles Dickens, the need for contact with the audience is there until the end, but it is satisfied in new and more direct ways. Thus, most strikingly, the notorious public readings. When, late in his life, Dickens reads from *Oliver Twist*, he is more in control of his audience, more exquisitely responsive to that audience, seated right there in the hall, than he could ever have been while writing and publishing the novel. But the script he would use for such public reading looks almost like Dickens edited by Austen. In the "Sikes and Nancy" script, for instance, there is a colloquy between Fagin and Noah Claypole in which nineteen speeches are included. None of the speeches is tagged, and the only authorial comment is one medial "leaning over the table." In the original version of the colloquy (the opening of Chapter 45 of *Oliver Twist*) there are twenty-seven speeches (none very long) and all but three have some sort of tag attached. We may say the tags are deleted from the "Sikes and Nancy" adaptation because they were, for the author, psychologically redundant: no need for the *inquit, ergo sum* tag when the author is physically there, presenting something like a mono-polylogue. On the other hand, we might read the script version of this colloquy and think, yes, that is the way the late (or mature or dark) Dickens would likely have written the scene for publication in the sixties or late fifties. And we may then turn this observation around: perhaps the public readings (which began late in 1853, the year *Bleak House* was completed) were one of the things allowing Dickens to develop a colder style in the second half of his career. That is, perhaps Dickens learned to satisfy his need for contact through bouts of physical confrontation with his audience and thus had less need for such indirect contact as the heavy use of tags in his writings for publication.[7] One might say that the Dickensian need to charm and control becomes partially ritualized in the second half of the author's career: it is indulged, expressed in periods of intense contact with his audience, and therefore need not be indulged as heavily as it had been through diffused, indirect contact with his readers.

"One might say." Much virtue in a "might." We end with speculation, but of course we have speculated all the way through, added hypothesis to hypothesis: our microscope is a modified crystal ball, and we have restricted our field of vision not so that we could have certainty rather than speculation but so that we could have more things to speculate about: we simplify to complicate, choosing to simplify by looking first at style rather than archetypal story pattern or socio-economic background, or authorial psychology. Word, sentence, image, symbol, chapter, structure, narrator, author, reader, genre, society, era: each complex, each complexly relatable to each of the others. Our criticism begins not with the act of combining but, as I have said, with the act of separation, so that the undistracted viewer can take in more of the complexity of some part of the whole (whatever one takes the whole to be). According to taste, we make the decision to restrict ourselves initially to this rather than that. In one way this decision according to taste is a very momentous decision (the present book, I remind you, is a test of your taste for one sort of initial restriction) and in another sense not. We can connect any one aspect of a book with any other aspect; we preclude consideration of no $x$ by starting with $y$. On the other hand, we are more likely to make some connections than others, and we are never going to make every connection that might be made or every connection it might give us pleasure to make. Whenever we start examining a work the world lies all before us: there is no place we can't get to from the first road we choose, but in no case are we going to reach all the places we would like to visit. We should choose the first road not because of the places it leads to but because it seems pleasant in itself.

# *Appendix 1. Narrative Tense and Direct Quotation: A Brief Anthology*

During the last few centuries writers of English have tended to assume that casual or colloquial or semiliterate storytellers associate direct quotation of characters with narration in the present tense. I collect here a number of passages where an author either shows such a storyteller favoring the present tense for speech-tags or in which a sophisticated writer, finding an unstudied style appropriate, himself uses present tense tags. The bearing upon our main study of this association of present tense and speech-tags is discussed in chapter two, pp. 79–80. I do, by the way, think novelists have been fundamentally right about the way tenses are employed in casual narration; it will be good, however, to remind ourselves that we are mainly concerned not with the way in which certain speakers of English have actually used tenses but with the way novelists and other writers of English seem to have thought those speakers used tenses.

Having explained that, I must go on to explain one or two other things and shall then begin to quote. First, it is only occasionally that we encounter imitations of colloquial storytelling where the pattern is simply and consistently that all narrative verbs shall be in the past tense except for speech-tag verbs, which are always in the present tense. Once in a while we find something *almost* that simple, but not often enough to claim that is the rule. We do better, I believe, to think of a colloquial tale (as it is presented to us in literary works) as something where a sense of excitement, involvement, resurrection of the past, may lead some storytellers to put virtually all the narrative in the present tense, while others will leave all of it in the past tense. The important point, the thing that does have some claims to rulehood, is that if there is present tense narration in such a tale, the tag-verbs will share in it: proximity to direct quotation is the thing most likely to pull narration into the present tense.

Second, a point which may have some bearing on the pattern we are illustrating here and which is at the very least distracting: in colloquial English of the past several centuries there is a tendency to level the first person singular with the third person singular of the present indicative; thus, in *Pickwick Papers*, Joe the fat boy's "I wants to make your flesh creep." (chap. 8, p. 102).[1] Now Joe's sort of usage creates no particular difficulties for us; what does cause trouble is a complication we notice when we move to speakers who are somewhat above Joe on the sociolinguistic scale. Many such speakers (both in life and in fiction) seem to "fall into" the use of the first person singular *-s only* when narrating an anecdote set in the past; elsewhere (that is, whenever the present indicative is not a historical present) they employ a standard English form without final *-s*. (For instance, "So finally I goes to him . . ." but "I just love the place. I go there every chance I get.") It has been argued that this restricted, "anecdotal" employment of *-s* as a first person singular ending indicates the existence of a special narrational tense: a tense in which the speaker feels a presentness in the action being recalled but at the same time senses that this action can also be thought of as in the past. Having this double perception, the speaker chooses a present tense verbal ending but a rule for the use of that ending (first person singular and third person singular are identical) which belongs to the past tense.[2] This explanation is at the very least ingenious. For our purposes, though, the point to bear in mind is that even when a restricted use of the anecdotal first person *-s* is analyzed in this way, the speaker who says "so I tells him" still suggests a greater sense of *hereness* in the action described than he does when he selects the common stylistic alternative, a simple past tense ("so I told him"). It is also worth noting that (at least according to Levin's study, cited above) the various speech-tag verbs (*say* above all) are the ones most likely to be used with this "vulgar historical present" first person *-s* in modern spoken English. It is *say*, the basic tag-verb, which is most often pulled into, or at least *toward*, presentness.

Now, to the anthology. I shall start with a nice, clear example, an anecdote which appeared in the 1684 volume *Oxford Jests Refined and Enlarged* . . . .

> A patient man coming home from work, but it seems did not bring home to his Shrewish Wife so much money as she expected; with that she flew about his ears, and did so jole him! Good wife, says he, be quiet, for I would willingly wear my bands without cuffs, if you please.[3]

Fairly informal writing: the finite verbs of the narrative section (*did*, *expected*, *flew*, *did*) are in the past except for the tag-verb: *says*. Dorothy Wordsworth distributes tenses in much the same way in her Grasmere Journal entry for 23 June 1800:

> An old man saw me just after I had crossed the stepping stones, and was going through a copse—'Ho, wherever were you going?' 'To Elterwater Bridge'—'Why,' says he, 'it's well I saw you: ye were gane to Little Langdale by Wrynose,' and several other places which he ran over with a mixture of triumph, good-nature and wit—'It's well I saw you or you'd ha' been lost.' . . .[4]

Here it is interesting to notice that the present tense is used with a direct quotation *inquit*, but a temporary return to summary rather than direct quotation means a return to the narrative past ("which he *ran* over"): for this time, at least, only *ipsissima verba* have the power to bring narrational presentness.

Now artistic imitations of unstudied narrative. In Beaumont's *The Knight of the Burning Pestle* (first published 1613, and probably written about six years earlier) Nell, the Citizen's Wife, moves from past tense to present when she comes to *say* and direct quotation:

> I shall ne'er forget him, when we had lost our child (you know it was stray'd almost, alone, to Puddlewharf, and the criers were abroad for it, and there it had drown'd itself but for a sculler); Rafe, was the most comfortablest to me. "Peace, mistress," says he, "let it go; I'll get you another as good." Did he not, George; did he not say so?[5]

From our own century we may cite Mr. Casey's disruptive anecdote in Joyce's *Portrait of the Artist as a Young Man*:

> —It was down in Arklow one day. We were down there at a meeting and after the meeting was over we had to make our way to the railway station through the crowd. Such booing and baaing, man, you never heard. They called us all the names in the world. Well there was one old lady, and a drunken old harridan she was surely, that paid all her attention to me. She kept dancing along beside me in the mud bawling and screaming into my face: *Priesthunter! The Paris Funds! Mr. Fox! Kitty O'Shea!*
>
> —And what did you do, John? asked Mr. Dedalus.
>
> —I let her bawl away, said Mr. Casey. It was a cold day and to keep up my heart I had (saving your presence, ma'am) a quid of Tullamore in my mouth and sure I couldn't say a word in any case because my mouth was full of tobacco juice.
>
> —Well, John?
>
> —Well. I let her bawl away, to her heart's content, *Kitty O'Shea* and the rest of it till at last she called that lady a name that I won't sully this Christmas board nor your ears, ma'am, nor my own lips by repeating.

> He paused. Mr. Dedalus, lifting his head from the bone, asked:
>
> —And what did you do, John?
>
> —Do! said Mr. Casey. She stuck her ugly old face up at me when she said it and I had my mouth full of tobacco juice. I bent down and *Phth!* says I to her like that.
>
> He turned and made the act of spitting.
>
> —*Phth!* says I to her like that, right into her eye.
>
> He clapped a hand to his eye and gave a hoarse scream of pain.
>
> —*O Jesus, Mary and Joseph!* says she. *I'm blinded! I'm blinded and drownded!*
>
> He stopped in a fit of coughing and laughter, repeating:
>
> —*I'm blinded entirely.*[6]

Mr. Casey casts his narrative in the past tense but moves to the present when tagging direct quotations. The one exception here is the first quotation from his adversary, which is introduced by participial rather than finite forms of speech verbs ("She kept dancing along beside me in the mud bawling and screaming into my face. . .").

In the following passage from *Moll Flanders* there is, notwithstanding the Old Convention paragraphing and lack of typographical differentiation between *ipsissima verba* and other forms of quotation, a nice (and by now, I trust, somewhat familiar) differentiation by tense between tag-verbs for direct quotations and tag-verbs for other forms of quotation. (I have italicized important verbs here and in subsequent passages.)

> Accordingly after dinner, he very gravely *says* to me, his sisters being all by, Mrs. Betty, I must ask a favour of you. What's that? *says* the second sister. Nay, sister, *says* he, very gravely, if you can't spare Mrs. Betty to-day, any other time will do. Yes, they *said*, they could spare her well enough, and the sisters *beg'd* pardon for asking. Well, but, *says* the eldest sister, you must tell Mrs. Betty what it is. . . .[7]

Like Moll Flanders, Huckleberry Finn often displays a nice

sensitivity to the difference between indirect and direct quotation:

> Everybody *said* it was a real beautiful oath, and *asked* Tom if he got it out of his own head. He *said* some of it, but the rest was out of pirate-books, and every gang that was high-toned had it.
>
> Some *thought* it would be good to kill the *families* of boys that told the secrets. Tom *said* it was a good idea, so he *took* a pencil and *wrote* it in. Then Ben Rogers *says*:
>
> "Here's Huck Finn. He hain't got no family; what you going to do 'bout him?"[8]

But neither of these masters of colloquial narration—neither Moll Flanders nor Huck Finn—uses the narrative present exclusively or inevitably for direct quotation tag-verbs. There is no "all and only" here, but rather something like a strong gravitational pull. In the following passage, for instance, "presentness" washes back from the anticipated direct quotation to affect not only Huck's tag-verb but the next closest narrative verb as well:

> I *had* just one little glimpse of the old gentleman when he *come* in; then the bed *hid* him. Mrs. Phelps she *jumps* for him, and *says*:
>
> "Has he come?"[9]

(It seems doubtful, by the way, that the liveliness of the action described is the major explanation of the form *jumps*: on the next page, for instance, a narrative paragraph begins "He *sprung* to the window . . .") I turn back to *Moll Flanders* to show an additional degree of blurriness: in the sentences below the first direct quotation tag is in the past tense and several non-tag-verbs in the present. (Moll's emotions at this moment do not explain her usage: we must speak about strong tendencies rather than absolute rules.)

> This gentleman *had* now fir'd his inclination, as much as he *had* my vanity, and as if he had found that he had an opportunity, and was sorry he did not take hold of it, he

*comes* up again in about half an hour, and *falls* to work with me again just as he did before, only with a little less introduction.

And first when he *entered* the room he *turn'd* about, and *shut* the door. Mrs. Betty, *said* he, I fancy'd before, some body was coming up stairs, but it was not so; however, *adds* he, if they find me in the room with you, they shan't catch me a kissing of you. I *told* him I did not know who should be coming up stairs, for I believed there was no body in the house but the cook, and the other maid, and they never came up those stairs. Well, my dear, *says* he, 'tis good to be sure however; and so he *sits* down and we *began* to talk. . . .[10]

Now of course what most concerns us in all this is Charles Dickens's sense that popular or informal speech tends to bring tag-verbs into the present tense more often than other narrative verbs. That sense is there: one finds something quite like the *Huckleberry Finn* pattern of tense distribution when Inspector Wield (the model for Inspector Bucket of *Bleak House*) narrates one of his adventures in "Three 'Detective' Anecdotes":

"Well, sir, we put our pipes aboard, and we *drank* our half-and-half, and *sat* a-talking, very sociably, when the young man *says*, 'You must excuse me stopping very long,' he *says*, 'because I'm forced to go home in good time. I must be at work all night.' 'At work all night?' *says* I. 'You ain't a baker?' 'No,' he *says*, laughing, 'I ain't a baker.' 'I thought not,' *says* I, 'you haven't the looks of a baker.' 'No,' *says* he, 'I'm a glove-cleaner.'

"I never was more astonished in my life than when I *heard* them words come out of his lips. 'You're a glove-cleaner, are you?' *says* I. 'Yes,' he *says*, 'I am.'"

[*UT*, p. 505]

Elsewhere in Dickens, colloquial narrators will put all or almost all of their narration in the present tense. Thus, this presentation of a tramp telling a story to a sympathetic audience:

"So as I'm a standing at the pump in the market, blest if there don't come up a Beadle, and he ses, 'Mustn't stand there,' he ses. 'Why not?' I ses. 'No beggars allowed in this town,' he ses. 'Who's a beggar?' I ses. 'You are,' he ses. . . ."

["Tramps," *UT*, p. 110]

It is true that Dickensian characters who narrate in the present tense also tend to include a great deal of dialogue in their tales (for example, Sarah Gamp), but it seems better to be conservative here and attribute the use of tenses in "So as I'm a standing at the pump in the market, blest if there don't come up a Beadle . . ." not to any special sense of the presentness of quoted dialogue but rather to the "uraltvolkstumlich" tendency to think of *all* that is being recalled—words, but also things and deeds—as present.[11] Still, even disregarding such passages as naive historical present and therefore not good evidence of a sense of special presentness in directly quoted speech, we do have things like the Inspector Wield narrative to suggest Dickens felt, as did Twain and Defoe, that direct quotation had, for the casual or uneducated speaker, a privileged vividness. And we have as perhaps our most amusing (as well as our longest) example Sam Weller's memorable story of the sausagemaker and his wife:

"He *was* the master o' that 'ere shop, sir, and the inwenter o' the patent-never-leaving'-off sassage steam ingine, as *ud* swaller up a pavin' stone if you put it too near, and grind it into sassages as easy as if it was a tender young babby. Werry proud o' that machine he *was*, as it *was* nat'ral he should be, and *he'd* stand down in the celler a lookin' at it wen it *was* in full play, till he *got* quite melancholy with joy. A wery happy man he'd ha' been, sir, in the procession o' that ere ingine and two more lovely hinfants besides, if it hadn't been for his wife, who *was* a most owdacious wixin. She *was* always a follerin' him about, and dinnin' in his ears, 'till at last he *couldn't* stand it no longer. 'I'll tell you what it is, my dear,' he *says* one day; 'if you persewere in this here sort of amusement,' he *says*, 'I'm blessed if I don't go away to 'Merriker; and that's all about it.' 'You're a idle willin,' *says* she, 'and I wish the 'Merrikins joy of their bargain.' Arter wich she *keeps* on abusin' of him for half an hour, and then *runs* into the little parlour behind the shop, *sets* to a screamin', *says* he'll be the death on her, and *falls* in a fit, which *lasts* for three good hours—one o' them fits wich is all screamin' and kickin'. Well, next mornin', the husband *was* missin'. He *hadn't* taken nothin' from the till,—hadn't even put on his great-coat—so it *was* quite clear he warn't gone to 'Merriker. *Didn't* come back next day; *didn't* come back next week; Missis *had* bills printed, sayin' that, if he'd come back, he should be forgiven everythin' (which was very liberal, seein' that he hadn't done nothin' at all); canals *was* dragged, and for two months artervards, wenever a body *turned* up, it *was* carried, as a reg'lar thing, straight off to the sassage shop. Hows'ever, none on 'em *answered*; so they *gave* out that he'd run away, and she *kep* on the bis'ness. One Saturday night, a little thin old gen'l'm'n *comes* into the shop in a great passion and *says*, 'Are you the missis o' this here shop?' 'Yes, I am,' *says* she. 'Well, ma'am,' *says* he, 'then I've just looked in to say that me and my family ain't a goin' to be choked for nothin'; and more than that, Ma'am,' he *says* 'you'll allow me to observe, that as you don't use the primest parts of the meat in the manafacter o' sassages, I think you'd find beef come nearly as cheap as buttons.' 'As buttons, sir!' *says* she. 'Buttons, ma'am,' *says* the little old gentleman, unfolding a bit of paper, and shewin' twenty or thirty halves o' buttons. 'Nice seasonin' for sassages, is trousers' buttons, ma'am.' 'They're my husband's buttons!' [*says*] the widder, beginnin' to faint. 'What!' *screams* the little old gen'l'm'n, turnin' very pale. 'I see it all,' *says* the widder; 'in a fit of temporary insanity he rashly converted his-self into sassages!' And so he *had* sir,'' said Mr. Weller, looking steadily into Mr. Pickwick's horror-stricken countenance, ''or else *he'd* been draw'd into the ingine; but however that might *ha' been*, the little old gen'l'm'n, who *had been* remarkably partial to sassages all his life, *rushed* out o' the shop in a wild state, and *was* never heerd on artervards!"

[*PP*, chap. 31, pp. 423-24]

There is much to be learned here about domestic relations and forcemeats as well as narrative tenses. But I shall confine my remarks to the last of these. Sam's narration does not show a pure, "all and only" pattern: all the tag-verbs are in the present tense, but not all the other finite narrative verbs are in the past. It will be seen, though, that the gravitational pull analogy works quite well for Sam's narrative. Action is spoken about in the past tense until we have direct quotation and tag-verbs in the present tense. The melodramatic actions consequent on the exchange of speeches—felt to be closely tied to those speeches—which end the scene are narrated, like those speeches, in the present tense (*keeps*, *runs*, *sets*, *says*, *falls*, *lasts*). Comes the dawn, and we have a new episode which is narrated in the past tense until we come up to the old gentleman's entrance into the shop. Here the "pull" of direct quotation makes itself felt one narrative verb early: in "*comes* into the shop in a great passion and *says*," the entering and speaking are thought of as a single action. The rest of the narrative verbs in this scene are present tense tags, and the conclusion of the story contains neither direct quotation nor the narrational present. Having concluded this analysis of Sam's use of tenses, I must say that I hear the words of Sam's father: "vether it's worth while goin' through so much to learn so little, as the charity-boy said ven he got to the end of the alphabet, is a matter o' taste." So it is. My point here is that for centuries English colloquial narration has had a tendency (or so at least writers have believed) to distribute tenses in a way that suggests that quoted words are more fully "present" than described actions. Dickens on occasion imitated this distribution of tenses, and I assume that he had his intuitions about the meaning, the psychological motivation, of this distribution.[12]

# *Appendix 2. On the Counts*

Below are the data upon which I've based the tables in chapter three. The first part of this appendix is a key to the various runs of 100 directly quoted speeches I have examined. Because almost all of these runs begin with the first directly quoted speech in a given chapter, and continue without interruption until the hundredth such quotation is reached, I've identified runs by simply giving the chapters in which they start. Where there is a more complicated sort of run, I have of course pointed this out. The tables in part 2 of this appendix give numbers of suspensions and untagged quotations for each run; they repeat from my third chapter (but now under the more formal heading [arithmetic] "mean") the average percentages of untagged quotations and suspensions in the runs from each work; and they also present, for each of those arithmetic means, the standard deviation ($\sigma$) and standard error. I have also given the means, standard deviations, and standard errors of the means for my 40 runs representing each of those larger "populations," Early Dickens, Late Dickens, and Others (that is, table 3 and table 4 novels).

The statistical evidence for differences between the quoting styles of early and late Dickens, and even between some of those smaller populations, individual novels, looks good, and I am very pleased to point this out. But though I find these results reassuring, I do not want to suggest that the figures below show more than they do. I recommend a conservative and limited use of these tables: any of the numerical differences is far better employed by the critic as a stimulus or point of departure or partial check than as a proof that a certain literary interpretation is right.[1] This caveat may be in part the expression of an innumerate's prejudices, but it is not entirely the product of fear and ignorance. We must remember what the numbers are about and what we are about. Above all, we should recall that we are primarily concerned with differences to which readers respond and not simply differences which exist: it is worth repeating that data drawn from texts, no matter how precise, cannot tell us anything about *responses* to stylistic features.[2] Strictly speaking, we could continue to be objective and scientific only by trying to correlate data drawn from texts with data drawn from reader reactions to those texts. If we are not going to do that (or if our data about reader responses are nothing more scientific than the assertions about Old Dickensians made in chapter three) and if, at the same time, we are not going to discard our statistical findings altogether, we need a good, commonsensical working assumption: the larger a difference, the more likely that readers respond to it.

My caveat about the wholesome use of the figures below also has something to do with the figures themselves. I have reexamined enough of my collection of 14,300 quotations to know that I am not an infallible counter (though statisticians, it is comforting to note, expect some errors in data collection). It should be remembered that the editions I have used are not the ones read by Dickens's contemporaries, and it is possible an occasional "said he" has been deleted in a reprinting. One must recall that my definition of the suspended quotation is a *working* definition and somewhat arbitrary: no doubt some of our numerical contrasts would be more dramatic, and others less so, if I had elected to count in four-word suspensions or to exclude all suspensions with fewer than seven words.

Having confessed my suspicions about the accuracy of my counts, I will begin this paragraph affirmatively. In the great majority of cases one has little difficulty deciding whether something is or is not a suspension of at least five words, is or is not an untagged direct quotation. For the rest, I have tried to be consistent. "Dramatic" speech-prefixes (such as we found in Peacock, Surtees, and Thackeray) count as tags. I take as speeches statements which are formally indistinguishable from direct discourse even if the tag-verb attached to them is *think* rather than a verb of utterance (for example, " 'Yes,' thought he, 'that is but just.' "). I disregard notes and letters. I disregard quotations within quotations and quotations within letters, if the letters or primary quotations are reasonably brief. ("Reasonably" is not a technical term.) When a character is quoted in two consecutive paragraphs, and the first of the paragraphs ends or the second begins with an authorial comment, I do not consider that comment a suspension: such paragraphing seems designed precisely to avoid the effect of authorial interruption. "Old-fashioned" indirect quotations within quotation marks are passed over. Hyphenated forms are treated as single words. And so forth. Consistency does seem important here, though I suspect perfection has again eluded me. With those very few things which called for some sort of decision and seemed likely to prove unique, I followed common sense if it seemed disposed to lead and otherwise chose the interpretation which went against the case I was trying to argue.

## 1. Key

Early Dickens

*Pickwick Papers:* run *a*, chap. 9; run *b*, chap. 23; run *c*, chap. 33; run *d*, chap. 47; run *e*, chap. 50.

*Oliver Twist:* run *a*, chap. 3; run *b*, chap. 21; run *c*, chap. 31; run *d*, chap. 36; run *e*, chap. 51.

*Nicholas Nickleby*; run *a*, chap. 3; run *b*, chap. 22; run *c*, chap. 38; run *d*, chap. 47; run *e*, chap. 59.

*The Old Curiosity Shop:* run *a*, chap. 11; run *b*, chap. 20; run *c*, chap. 30; run *d*, chap. 46; run *e*, chap. 60.
*Barnaby Rudge:* run *a*, chap. 12; run *b*, chap. 28; run *c*, chap. 40; run *d*, chap. 53; run *e*, chap. 73.
*Martin Chuzzlewit:* run *a*, chap. 6; run *b*, chap. 28; run *c*, chap. 30; run *d*, chap. 46; run *e*, chap. 51.
*Dombey and Son:* run *a*, chap. 2; run *b*, chap. 9; run *c*, chap. 25; run *d*, chap. 38; run *e*, chap. 51.
*David Copperfield:* run *a*, chap. 10; run *b*, chap. 27; run *c*, chap. 29; run *d*, chap. 42; run *e*, chap. 59.

## Late Dickens

*Bleak House:* run *a*, chap. 6; run *b*, chap. 19; run *c*, chap. 30; run *d*, chap. 34; run *e*, chap. 58; run *f*, chap. 60. [Runs *a*, *c*, and *f* come from Esther's part of the novel, the other three runs from the unnamed narrator's sections. Because I thought some readers might want to compare (or begin to compare) the quoting styles of the two, I chose samples rather less randomly in *Bleak House* than in other novels and made sure the two parts of the book were equally represented. In one of the runs, *e*, I was forced to skip over some intervening Esther-chapters in order to include one-hundred quotations by the other, nameless narrator: *e* begins with chapter 58, continues until the end of that chapter (sixty-one speeches directly quoted), and resumes with chapter 63.]
*Hard Times:* run *a*, I, chap. 4; run *b*, I, chap. 9; run *c*, II, chap. 1; run *d*, II, chap. 6; run *e*, II, chap. 9; run *f*, III, chap. 4.
*Little Dorrit:* run *a*, I, chap. 2; run *b*, I, chap. 11; run *c*, I, chap. 24; run *d*, II, chap. 15; run *e*, II, chap. 18; run *f*, II, chap. 27.
*A Tale of Two Cities:* run *a*, I, chap. 5; run *b*, II, chap. 6; run *c*, II, chap. 13; run *d*, III, chap. 2; run *e*, III, chap. 11.
*Great Expectations:* run *a*,, chap. 3; run *b*, chap. 27; run *c*, chap. 38; run *d*, chap. 44; run *e*, chap. 46; run *f*, chap. 52. [Run *d* and run *e* are a bit too close together: we find only ninety speeches in the *d* run before we are into *e*'s territory. To fill out *d*, I have included the last ten speeches of chapter 43.]
*Our Mutual Friend:* run *a*, I, chap. 7; run *b*, I, chap. 12; run *c*, II, chap. 12; run *d*, III, chap. 12; run *e*, III, chap. 13; run *f*, IV, chap. 11.
*The Mystery of Edwin Drood:* run *a*, chap. 2; run *b*, chap. 7; run *c*, chap. 10; run *d*, chap. 15; run *e*, chap. 23.

## Other Nineteenth-Century Novels

*Waverley:* run *a*, chap. 18; run *b*, chap. 30; run *c*, chap. 38; run *d*, chap. 45; run *e*, chap. 59.
*Emma:* run *a*, I, chap. 7; run *b*, II, chap. 12; run *c*, III, chap. 10.
*Frankenstein:* almost all the novel's directly quoted speeches are included. My two-hundred-speech count begins one speech before "Letter 4."
*Vanity Fair:* run *a*, chap. 7; run *b*, chap. 28; run *c*, chap. 34; run *d*, chap. 48; run *e*, chap. 61.
*Jane Eyre:* run *a*, chap. 5; run *b*, chap. 17; run *c*, chap. 29.
*Wuthering Heights:* run *a*, chap. 9; run *b*, chap. 18; run *c*, the run of 100-speeches ending with the *last* in chapter 29.
*Mary Barton:* run *a*, chap. 4; run *b*, chap. 8; run *c*, chap. 18; run *d*, chap. 25; run *e*, chap. 33.
*Sybil:* run *a*, II, chap. 1; run *b*, II, chap. 13; run *c*, III, chap. 1; run *d*, IV, chap. 13; run *e*, VI, chap. 1.
*Yeast:* run *a*, chap. 3; run *b*, chap. 11; run *c*, chap. 16.
*Windsor Castle:* run *a*, II, chap. 2; run *b*, IV, chap. 1; run *c*, VI, chap. 4.
*Handley Cross:* run *a*, chap. 17; run *b*, chap. 22; run *c*, chap. 34.
*The Virginians:* run *a*, I, chap. 4; run *b*, I, chap. 22; run *c*, I, chap. 43; run *d*, II, chap. 8; run *e*, II, chap. 21.
*Adam Bede:* run *a*, chap. 3; run *b*, chap. 9; run *c*, chap. 20; run *d*, chap. 30; run *e*, chap. 49.
*The Woman in White:* run *a*, "The Story Begun by Walter Hartright," chap. 7; run *b*, "The Second Epoch," chap. 5; run *c*, "The Second Epoch," chap. 8; run *d*, "The Third Epoch," chap. 7; run *e*, "The Story Continued by Walter Hartright," chap. 2.
*Can You Forgive Her?:* run *a*, chap. 8; run *b*, chap. 21; run *c*, chap. 37; run *d*, chap. 69; run *e*, chap. 52.
*Alice's Adventures in Wonderland:* run *a*, chap. 7; run *b*, chap. 9; run *c*, chap. 11.

## 2. Tables

The figure in column A is the number of suspensions in a given run, and the figure in column B is the number of untagged quotations. The next column, "mean," presents the arithmetical means of the A and B figures for a particular work (presents, that is, the figures already given above in chapter three of this study). "$\sigma$" is Standard Deviation, and "S.E.M." is "Standard Error of the Mean" (Standard Deviation divided by the square root of the number of observations [here = number of "runs."] ).

Early Dickens

| *Work* | *Run* | *A* | *B* | *Mean* | *σ* | *S.E.M.* |
|---|---|---|---|---|---|---|
| *PP* | *a* | 25 | 6 | | | |
| | *b* | 28 | 8 | A:24.2 | 6.98 | 3.122 |
| | *c* | 12 | 2 | | | |
| | *d* | 29 | 4 | B:6.2 | 3.49 | 1.561 |
| | e | 27 | 11 | | | |
| *OT* | *a* | 23 | 2 | | | |
| | *b* | 44 | 0 | A:31.2 | 8.41 | 3.76 |
| | *c* | 28 | 2 | | | |
| | *d* | 26 | 6 | B:3.8 | 3.63 | 1.623 |
| | *e* | 35 | 9 | | | |
| *NN* | *a* | 26 | 0 | | | |
| | *b* | 21 | 6 | A:28.8 | 7.46 | 3.336 |
| | *c* | 34 | 5 | | | |
| | *d* | 39 | 7 | B:5.4 | 2.95 | 1.319 |
| | *e* | 24 | 7 | | | |
| *OCS* | *a* | 29 | 3 | | | |
| | *b* | 28 | 9 | A:35.4 | 7.02 | 3.139 |
| | *c* | 43 | 0 | | | |
| | *d* | 35 | 22 | B:7.4 | 8.79 | 3.93 |
| | *e* | 42 | 3 | | | |
| *BR* | *a* | 44 | 9 | | | |
| | *b* | 42 | 15 | A:37.2 | 7.19 | 3.215 |
| | *c* | 28 | 13 | | | |
| | *d* | 31 | 9 | B:11.6 | 2.61 | 1.167 |
| | *e* | 41 | 12 | | | |
| *MC* | *a* | 35 | 11 | | | |
| | *b* | 26 | 16 | A:30.0 | 7.28 | 3.256 |
| | *c* | 19 | 11 | | | |
| | *d* | 35 | 4 | B:10.4 | 4.28 | 1.914 |
| | *e* | 35 | 10 | | | |
| *DS* | *a* | 14 | 12 | | | |
| | *b* | 34 | 4 | A:31.0 | 10.05 | 4.494 |

| *Work* | *Run* | *A* | *B* | *Mean* | *σ* | *S.E.M.* |
|---|---|---|---|---|---|---|
| | *c* | 31 | 3 | | | |
| | *d* | 40 | 5 | B:5.8 | 3.56 | 1.592 |
| | *e* | 36 | 5 | | | |
| *DC* | *a* | 24 | 10 | | | |
| | *b* | 21 | 11 | A:25.6 | 4.39 | 1.963 |
| | *c* | 28 | 6 | | | |
| | *d* | 32 | 8 | B:9.0 | 2.00 | .894 |
| | *e* | 23 | 10 | | | |

Late Dickens

| *Work* | *Run* | *A* | *B* | *Mean* | *σ* | *S.E.M.* |
|---|---|---|---|---|---|---|
| *BH* | *a* | 25 | 11 | | | |
| | *b* | 23 | 7 | A:21.0 | 6.16 | 2.515 |
| | *c* | 14 | 28 | | | |
| | *d* | 30 | 30 | B:24.7 | 13.17 | 5.377 |
| | *e* | 19 | 42 | | | |
| | *f* | 15 | 30 | | | |
| *HT* | *a* | 18 | 17 | | | |
| | *b* | 18 | 36 | A:20.0 | 4.43 | 1.809 |
| | *c* | 22 | 16 | | | |
| | *d* | 21 | 40 | B:26.7 | 10.06 | 4.107 |
| | *e* | 14 | 28 | | | |
| | *f* | 27 | 23 | | | |
| *LD* | *a* | 16 | 40 | | | |
| | *b* | 23 | 38 | A:21.8 | 3.06 | 1.249 |
| | *c* | 21 | 30 | | | |
| | *d* | 24 | 18 | B:31.3 | 7.84 | 3.201 |
| | *e* | 24 | 33 | | | |
| | *f* | 23 | 29 | | | |
| *TTC* | *a* | 12 | 43 | | | |
| | *b* | 18 | 39 | A:17.4 | 3.12 | 1.395 |
| | *c* | 20 | 39 | | | |
| | *d* | 19 | 37 | B:39.6 | 2.19 | .979 |
| | *e* | 18 | 40 | | | |
| *GE* | *a* | 22 | 12 | | | |
| | *b* | 29 | 36 | A:21.3 | 4.41 | 1.800 |
| | *c* | 23 | 25 | | | |
| | *d* | 18 | 27 | B:29.0 | 7.04 | 2.874 |

| *Work* | *Run* | *A* | *B* | *Mean* | *σ* | *S.E.M.* |
|---|---|---|---|---|---|---|
| | *e* | 19 | 38 | | | |
| | *f* | 17 | 36 | | | |
| *OMF* | *a* | 13 | 33 | | | |
| | *b* | 22 | 39 | A:19.0 | 3.16 | 1.290 |
| | *c* | 20 | 33 | | | |
| | *d* | 19 | 39 | B:33.0 | 10.90 | 4.450 |
| | *e* | 21 | 12 | | | |
| | *f* | 19 | 42 | | | |
| *ED* | *a* | 13 | 60 | | | |
| | *b* | 11 | 50 | A:13.8 | 6.54 | 2.925 |
| | *c* | 22 | 30 | | | |
| | *d* | 18 | 28 | B:46.4 | 16.70 | 7.468 |
| | *e* | 5 | 64 | | | |

## Other Nineteenth-Century Novels

| *Work* | *Run* | *A* | *B* | *Mean* | *σ* | *S.E.M.* |
|---|---|---|---|---|---|---|
| *Waverley* | *a* | 6 | 61 | | | |
| | *b* | 9 | 40 | A:14.0 | 9.03 | 4.038 |
| | *c* | 18 | 24 | | | |
| | *d* | 28 | 26 | B:39.8 | 15.47 | 6.918 |
| | *e* | 9 | 48 | | | |
| *Emma* | *a* | 5 | 53 | A:8.7 | 7.23 | 4.174 |
| | *b* | 4 | 36 | B:41.3 | 10.12 | 5.843 |
| | *c* | 17 | 35 | | | |
| *Frankenstein* | *a* | 11 | 34 | A:9.0 | | |
| | *b* | 7 | 29 | B:31.5 | | |
| *Vanity Fair* | *a* | 16 | 16 | | | |
| | *b* | 23 | 7 | A:19.8 | 3.56 | 1.592 |
| | *c* | 23 | 3 | | | |
| | *d* | 21 | 3 | B:7.2 | 4.67 | 2.088 |
| | *e* | 16 | 7 | | | |
| *Jane Eyre* | *a* | 1 | 65 | A:4.7 | 3.51 | 2.026 |
| | *b* | 8 | 52 | B:55.7 | 8.15 | 4.705 |
| | *c* | 5 | 50 | | | |
| *Wuthering Heights* | *a* | 14 | 28 | A:16.7 | 3.7 | 2.136 |
| | *b* | 21 | 2 | B:10.0 | 15.68 | 9.055 |
| | *c* | 15 | 0 | | | |

| *Work* | *Run* | *A* | *B* | *Mean* | *σ* | *S.E.M.* |
|---|---|---|---|---|---|---|
| *Mary Barton* | *a* | 7 | 50 | | | |
| | *b* | 8 | 52 | A:8.8 | 3.4 | 1.521 |
| | *c* | 5 | 37 | | | |
| | *d* | 14 | 35 | B:45.0 | 8.28 | 3.703 |
| | *e* | 10 | 51 | | | |
| *Sybil* | *a* | 13 | 26 | | | |
| | *b* | 13 | 30 | A:11.6 | 4.51 | 2.017 |
| | *c* | 4 | 32 | | | |
| | *d* | 12 | 29 | B:28.2 | 3.19 | 1.427 |
| | *e* | 16 | 24 | | | |
| *Yeast* | *a* | 2 | 62 | A:6.0 | 5.29 | 3.054 |
| | *b* | 12 | 46 | B:60.0 | 13.12 | 7.575 |
| | *c* | 4 | 72 | | | |
| *Windsor Castle* | *a* | 12 | 1 | A:11.0 | 1.73 | .999 |
| | *b* | 12 | 0 | B:0.3 | .71 | .410 |
| | *c* | 9 | 0 | | | |
| *Handley Cross* | *a* | 46 | 5 | A:44.0 | 3.5 | 2.020 |
| | *b* | 46 | 5 | B:3.7 | 2.31 | 1.334 |
| | *c* | 40 | 1 | | | |
| *The Virginians* | *a* | 20 | 17 | | | |
| | *b* | 9 | 27 | A:13.8 | 4.76 | 2.131 |
| | *c* | 15 | 14 | | | |
| | *d* | 9 | 19 | B:19.2 | 4.82 | 2.154 |
| | *e* | 16 | 19 | | | |
| *Adam Bede* | *a* | 19 | 40 | | | |
| | *b* | 19 | 35 | A:25.0 | 6.63 | 2.966 |
| | *c* | 35 | 16 | | | |
| | *d* | 27 | 24 | B:25.6 | 11.72 | 5.240 |
| | *e* | 25 | 13 | | | |
| *The Woman in White* | *a* | 8 | 31 | | | |
| | *b* | 9 | 34 | A:7.4 | 1.82 | .812 |
| | *c* | 5 | 58 | | | |
| | *d* | 6 | 52 | B:43.8 | 11.10 | 5.142 |
| | *e* | 9 | 44 | | | |
| *Can You Forgive Her?* | *a* | 11 | 34 | | | |
| | *b* | 9 | 70 | A:9.8 | 1.30 | .582 |
| | *c* | 8 | 64 | | | |

| *Work* | *Run* | *A* | *B* | *Mean* | *σ* | *S.E.M.* |
|---|---|---|---|---|---|---|
| | *d* | 10 | 35 | B:51.2 | 16.42 | 7.344 |
| | *e* | 11 | 53 | | | |
| *Alice's Adven-* | *a* | 14 | 0 | A:14.3 | .50 | .291 |
| *tures in Won-* | b | 15 | 4 | B:1.3 | 2.31 | 1.334 |
| *derland* | *c* | 14 | 0 | | | |

For my larger samplings of the "populations" Early Dickens (*Pickwick* through *Copperfield*) and Late Dickens (*Bleak House* through *The Mystery of Edwin Drood*) the corresponding figures are:

Suspensions

Early Dickens: mean, 30.4; standard deviation, 7.97; standard error of the mean, 1.260.

Late Dickens: mean, 19.4; standard deviation, 4.93; standard error of the mean, .780.

Untagged Quotations

Early Dickens: mean, 7.4; standard deviation, 4.73; standard error of the mean, .748.

Late Dickens: mean, 32.45; standard deviation, 12.14; standard error of the mean, 1.920.

For our third group of forty 100-speech runs—the non-Dickensian passages cited in table 3 of the third chapter—the corresponding figures are:

Suspensions: mean, 14.1; standard deviation, 10.65; standard error of the mean, 1.684.

Untagged Quotations: mean, 29.4; standard deviation, 21.35; standard error of the mean, 3.376.

# *Notes*

## CHAPTER ONE

1 Here the reader might well consider Stanley E. Fish's properly chastening paper, "What is Stylistics and Why are They Saying Such Terrible Things About It?" *Approaches to Poetics: Selected Papers from the English Institute*, edited with a Foreword by Seymour Chatman (New York, 1973), pp. 109-52.

2 I should explain, by the way, that I am excluding from stylistics—from the kind of stylistics I practice—the employment by an author of recognized tropes and figures in so far as these recognized tropes and figures are used for recognized or "officially sanctioned" ends: such uses of language are the proper objects of *rhetorical* analysis. Stylistics, in my sense, is the consideration of patterns in language which either are not described in handbooks of rhetoric or can be thought of as serving ends and having effects other than or in addition to those mentioned in the handbooks. Rhetoric is the use of linguistic patterns which have predetermined and thus translatable implications; stylistics is the study of linguistic patterns which do not, or in so far as they do not.

3 "Tradition and the Individual Talent," *The Sacred Wood: Essays on Poetry and Criticism* (London, 1920; reprinted 1960), pp. 49-50.

4 See *Adventures of Ideas* (New York, 1933), pp. 13-14.

5 See chap. 3 below.

6 *A Dictionary of Modern English Usage* (Oxford, 1944), pp. 292-93.

7 "Speech for the Royal Theatrical Fund," 1858. Quoted in Norman Page, *Speech in the English Novel* (London, 1973), p. 162.

8 A syntactically passive tag would of course be one where the quoted words become subject rather than object (" 'Yes,' was said

by him"). A semantically passive tag is one where the quoted words may be construed as the subject of an active construction in which the speaker of those words is indicated unambiguously but *en passant*—e.g., " 'Yes,' was George's emphatic reply." We may also consider as semantically passive tags those which direct attention to the reception rather than the production of a signal—e.g., " 'Yes,' she heard George say."

9 Stephen Ullmann, *Semantics: An Introduction to the Science of Meaning* (Oxford, 1962), p. 245. Jerrold J. Katz shows how the idea of semantic fields can be adapted to the rigorous requirements of a generative transformational grammar in his *Semantics* (New York, 1972), pp. 346–55. On the early history of the idea, see Suzanne Öhman's "Theories of the 'Linguistic Field,' " *Word* 9 (1953): 123–34.

There is at present no general agreement about either the terminology or boundaries of semantic field work. Generally, though, the semantic field idea has not been used to contrast literary idiolects with one another, nor has frequency of occurrence (rather than absolute occurrence or nonoccurrence) been considered relevant.

10 I quote from *The Collected Works of Oliver Goldsmith*, edited by Arthur Friedman (Oxford, 1966), vol. 4, p. 125.

A short count of the speeches occurring a little before the quoted exchange strengthens our impression of a rather high decibel level in *The Vicar of Wakefield.* I look at the one hundred directly quoted speeches which follow the opening of chap. 15 and find that *cry* is the most common tag-verb in that sample: it occurs forty-five times, *say* only six. (When Goldsmith's characters don't *cry* they *return*, *reply*, *continue*, *interrupt*, etc.) It is suggestive to compare these figures with some obtained from a look at three runs of one hundred tagged speeches each in *Nicholas Nickleby*. (On these, see chap. 2, n. 48 below.) In the *Nickleby* samples *say* is used 48 percent of the time, *cry* about 5 percent of the time: in effect, the proportions are reversed.

11 Goldsmith's practice, I should point out, does not represent a "standard" eighteenth-century punctuation in quite the way Dickens's practice is standard modern usage. In the eighteenth century authors and printers treat dialogue in a variety of ways. *Moll Flanders*, for instance, originally appeared without any marks of quotation separating dialogue from narration. (See James Southerland's "Textual and Biographical Note" to his edition of the

novel [Boston, 1959], p. xix, and the quotations from that edition in Appendix 1 of the present study.) In *The History of Sir Charles Grandison*, for instance, there are passages in which modern paragraphing rules seem to be followed and tags are optional—but quotation marks are not used. Thus:

> *I don't hit your fancy*, madam!
>
> Can you be a malicious man, Sir Hargrave?
>
> *You don't like my morals*, madam!
>
> And is this the way, Sir Hargrave, are these the means you take, to convince me that I ought to like them?
>
> Well, madam, you shall prove the mercy in me, you would not shew. You shall see that I cannot be a malicious man: And yet you have raised my pride. You shall find me a *moral* man.
>
> Then, Sir Hargrave, will I bless you from the bottom of my heart!
>
> [Letter XXIX; 7th edition, London, 1781]

On the other hand, when a Richardsonian correspondent wants to draw particular attention to the fact that a passage (especially a longish one) is an *ipsissima verba* quotation, quotation marks will be placed at the beginning of every line of that passage. For instance, from Letter XXVII:

> We then besought him to give an account of the glorious action, which had restored to all that knew her, the darling of our hearts.
>
> I will relate all, he said, in the first person, as nearly in his own words as possible, and will try to hit the coolness with which he told the agreeable story.
>
> 'You know, Sister, said he, the call I had to town. It was
> ' happy, that I yielded to your importunity to attend you hither.
>
> 'About two miles on this side Hounslow, I saw a chariot and
> ' six driving at a great rate. I also had ordered Jerry to drive
> ' pretty fast.
>
> 'The coachman seemed inclined to dispute the way with mine.
> ' This occasioned a few moments stop to both. I ordered my
> ' coachman to break the way. I don't love to stand upon trifles.
> ' My horses were fresh: I had not come far. . . .'

Such marks (almost never reproduced now—even by me!) are common in the age and stress the *fact* more than the purity of quotation. (Notice that the paragraph three inquit, the "said he," is not placed outside quotation marks.) One would guess that any possible combination of modern paragraphing and punctuating conventions, and conventions we have observed in *The Vicar of Wakefield*, *Grandison*, and *Moll Flanders*, and conventions involving italics or parentheses may be found somewhere in eighteenth-century English fiction.

It is of course worth remembering that English Romantic poetry (e.g., *Lyrical Ballads*) often used the line-initial quotation mark, and, perhaps more important, that most Victorian novelists, as well as an important part of their audience, knew contemporary French practice and thus would not think of the unsegregated inquit, for instance, as simply archaic.

12 For one classification of various "degrees of indirectness," see Page's *Speech in the English Novel*, chap. 2. Page's chapter (and, indeed, his book as a whole) will prove a most valuable supplement to the present work.

13 See Page, p. 29. Page is wrong, however, in suggesting that the practice is entirely abandoned by Dickens's period. Indeed, even the strict constructionist writers—the ones who think of quotation marks as guarantees of *ipsissima verba* quotation—may, once in a great while, employ broad constructionist patterns. Thus Dickens:

> Plornish became suspicious. Seemed to scent a creditor. Said, "Ah, Yes. Well. He didn't know what satisfaction *he* could give any gentleman respecting that family. What might it be about, now?"
>
> [*LD*, I, chap. 12, p. 138]

> Whether Mr. Tupman was already tired of retirement, or whether he was wholly unable to resist the eloquent appeal which was made to him, matters not, he did *not* resist at last.
>
> "It mattered little to him," he said, "where he dragged out the miserable remainder of his days: and since his friend laid so much stress upon his humble companionship, he was willing to share his adventures."
>
> [*PP*, chap. 9, p. 136]

It might be amusing to assemble all Dickens broad constructionist quotations (there can't be very many) and see what generalizations about them can be proposed. It seems a safe guess that in

Dickens broad constructionism is used to satirize speech which is not the verbally fresh overflow of powerful feeling. But can we describe the devices used and the targets more precisely?

When we think about broad constructionist and strict constructionist punctuation, we are of course considering the written or printed language of the nineteenth century as an object worthy of study in itself rather than as a mere representation of spoken language. The shift from one system of paragraphing and punctuation to another (more precisely, the establishment of one system of paragraphing and punctuation as normative) perhaps corresponds to nothing perceptible by someone *hearing* works of fiction read aloud; be that as it may, the shift seems to me a true and significant example of one of the two contrasting movements "of the interrelationship between . . . authorial and . . . reported speech" described by V. N. Voloshinov: "A language may strive to forge hard and fast boundaries for reported speech. In such a case, the patterns and their modifications serve to demarcate the reported speech as clearly as possible, to screen it from penetration by the author's intonations, and to condense and enhance its individual linguistic features." (*Marxism and the Philosophy of Language*, trans. Ladislav Matejka and I. R. Titunik [New York, 1973], p. 119.) I would say that the history of our language affords no clearer example of such a movement than the change in *written* English we are discussing.

14 There are some cases, however, where even greater liberties are taken. Notice how in the following passage from *The Heart of Midlothian* quotation marks set off both the *ipsissima verba* of a character using Scots and also a Standard English summary of that character's speech:

> "Hout, ay," said one of the boatmen, "there's the Caird's Cove; but we dinna tell the minister about it, and I am no sure if I can steer the boat to it, the bay is sae fu' o' shoals and sunk rocks."
>
> "Try," said Sir George, "and I will give you half-a-guinea."
>
> The old fellow took the helm, and observed, "that if they could get in, there was a steep path up from the beach, and half-an-hour's walk from thence to the Manse."
>
> "Are you sure you know the way?" said Butler to the old man.
>
> "I maybe kend it a wee better fifteen years syne, when Dandie Wilson was in the Frith wi' his clean-ganging lugger. . . . "
>
> [chap. 51, pp. 543–44]

15 On mixed forms of discourse, see Gertrude L. Schuelke, " 'Slipping' in Indirect Discourse," *American Speech* 33 (1958): 90-98, Mark Lambert, *Malory: Style and Vision in Le Morte Darthur* (New Haven and London, 1975), pp. 2-8, and Voloshinov, p. 132.

16 *Erlebte Rede* has been exhaustively discussed by twentieth-century stylisticians, and I am happy to announce that I will have almost nothing to say about it in the present book. For a good brief introduction to the subject, I recommend Graham Hough, *Style and Stylistics* (London, 1969), pp. 34-37.

17 Dickens is of course not simply analyzable in cinematic terms: his works probably had a good deal of influence on the development of film technique. See Sergei Eisenstein's lovely "Dickens, Griffith, and the Film Today," in *Film Form: Essays in Film Theory*, ed. and trans. Jay Leyda (New York, 1949; reprinted, Cleveland and New York, 1957, in *Film Form: Essays in Film Theory and the Film Sense*), pp. 195-255.

18 A novelist can also work the gothic vein—or a humorous one—by making the subject of a tag a voice rather than a person: in *OCS*, for instance, Dickens has "cried several voices . . ." on p. 351 and "said a voice . . ." on p. 355.

## CHAPTER TWO

1 Notice the importance of paragraphing here. Because of the initial and closing quotation marks, the reader sees from the first that this paragraph is to be taken as a single speech. Thus, when he actually reads through the paragraph word by word, he comes to the narrator's interjection with the knowledge that Mrs. Joe is not yet done speaking.

2 And Sterne, by the bye, surely holds the long-distance record for suspended quotations. Recall Uncle Toby's speech, which is interrupted in the twenty-first chapter of the first volume and not taken up again until the opening of vol. 2, chap. 6. (The edition quoted is James Aiken Work's [New York, 1940].)

3 See *The Flint and the Flame: The Artistry of Charles Dickens* (Columbia, Mo., 1963), p. 41. The passage (which I quote from Page's *Speech in the English Novel*) appears in Mamie Dickens, *My Father as I Recall Him* (New York, 1898), pp. 49-50.

4 An interesting exception here is a passage in Robert Roberts's *The Classic Slum: Salford Life in the First Quarter of the Century* (Baltimore, 1971). No one would think of this author as precious

or mannered, but notice how he presents a comment about an ex-prostitute:

> The moralists found it hard to forgive and they never forgot. "I wonder," sniffed one old neighbor to another, after hearing of the outbreak of the second world war, "I wonder if Mrs. J., with her husband away, will go on the game again like what she did last time?"
>
> [p. 22]

Roberts does not want us thinking about authorial manipulation of experience: he simply dislikes this moralizing neighbor very much and chooses the catchword suspension, just as he chooses the word *sniffed*, as a way to punish her. Roberts uses the device to serve purposes it served a century before, understands the powers of the device as a mid-Victorian understood them. See below.

5 Dickens is one such novelist, understands the specially intrusive character of an inquit or suspension introduced at a moment when the speaker is unlikely to pause heavily. Thus, in *Barnaby Rudge:*

> "There are strings," said Mr. Tappertit, flourishing his bread-and-cheese knife in the air, "in the human heart that had better not be wibrated. That's what's the matter."
>
> [p. 172]

This is the sort of effect someone like Stephen Booth understands so well when it occurs in verse. We assume that Simon does pause after "there are strings" and that the bread-and-cheese knife is something to be used upon those strings. When we have finished reading the passage, we realize we have misconstrued, misdivided the speech. But in the Dickensian context we react to our need to correct our first reading of the line by feeling that Sim has spoken in a grotesque, humorously and unintentionally ambiguous manner, not that the author has misled us. (Compare a less misleading —and less interesting—version of the speech which would, nonetheless, still be passable Dickens:

> "There are strings in the human heart," said Mr. Tappertit, flourishing his bread-and-cheese knife in the air, "that had better not be wibrated. That's what's the matter.")

In the following passage from *Dombey and Son*, the interruption of Edith's speech is only four words long, and thus, according to the rule we have devised, does not even qualify as a suspension. But notice how its position lends it considerable disruptive force:

> As Mrs. Skewton drew her purse out with a trembling hand, and eagerly fumbled for some money, which the other old woman greedily watched for—their heads all but touching, in their hurry and decrepitude—Edith interposed:
> "I have seen you," *addressing the old woman*, "before."
> [p. 575]

6 See *Castle Rackrent*, pp. 51–52; *Heart of Midlothian*, p. 442. Catchword suspensions could also be found in French writings:

> Accablé de sa majesté, je tombai à ses genoux, et lui demandai pardon de mes emportements. "Mon fils, me répondit-il avec " un accent si doux, que le remords entra dans mon âme, mon " fils, ce n'est pas pour moi-même que je vous ai réprimandé. . . .
> [Chateaubriand's *Atala* (*Atala—René*, Chronologie et préface par Pierre Reboul, Garnier-Flammarion [Paris, 1964], p. 118.)]

7 Dickens of course would come to know Bulwer-Lytton well and indeed gave Bulwer's name to the last of his children. The later Bulwer-Lytton was no longer the Regency exquisite, but Dickens could not have failed to be aware of *Pelham*, which was, among other things, the local irritation Carlyle scratched in *Sartor Resartus.*

8 See Marryat's "How to Write a Fashionable Novel" and also Ellen Moers's amusing account of the reception of *Vivian Grey* in *The Dandy: Brummell to Beerbohm* (New York, 1960; republished Lincoln, Neb., 1978), pp. 84–86. The second, third, and fourth chapters of Moers's book are very helpful background reading here.

9 See also, e.g., *Nicholas Nickleby*, pp. 131, 207.

Here again it seems to me important that we understand most novels as *written* language, not just transcribed speech: we know that in written language a false start can be eradicated, while in spoken language it can only be corrected. Thus when we have something like a catchword suspension in spoken language (or the imitation of spoken language) our impression is not likely to be that the quoter does not care whether he distorts the quoted sentences or not, but rather that he is momentarily overwhelmed by the number of things needing to be explained. For instance, the king in *All's Well that Ends Well* is clearly inundated by memories as he quotes the words of Bertram's father:

He would always say—
Methinks I hear him now; his plausive words
He scattered not in ears, but grafted them
To grow there and to bear—"Let me not live,"
(This his good melancholy oft began
On the catastrophe and heel of pastime,
When it was out) "Let me not live," quoth he,
"After my flame lacks oil, to be the snuff
Of younger spirits. . . ."

[I, 2, 52-60]

10 *Don Juan*, I. Byron is of course immensely important for an understanding of Regency attitudes. The publisher's puff for the about-to-be-published *Vivian Grey* declared, "It is said to be a sort of Don Juan in prose." (See Moers, p. 84.)

11 The best evidence here is the quotation of written rather than spoken words. Thus, for instance, the following passage in "A Curious Dance Round a Curious Tree," an article on the treatment of insanity written for *Household Words* by Dickens and W. H. Wills (1852). The quotation here seems to be from a work by an eighteenth-century physician, and no one reading the paragraph would suppose the doctor Wills and Dickens are quoting actually wrote the words "the skin being less liable to be injured" twice:

> "In cases of great fury and violence," says the amiable practitioner from whom I quote, "the patient should be kept in a dark room, confined by one leg, with metallic manacles on the wrist; the skin being less liable to be injured"—here the good doctor becomes especially considerate and mild—"the skin being less liable to be injured by the friction of polished metal than by that of linen or cotton."
>
> [*Charles Dickens' Uncollected Writings from Household Words*, 2 vols., edited with an Introduction and Notes by Harry Stone (Bloomington, 1968), 2: 383]

In *Pelham* (I.xii) Bulwer includes a fairly long letter of advice from the hero's mother. The letter is thus introduced:

> The next morning I received a letter from my mother.
> "My dear Henry," began my affectionate and incomparable parent—
> "MY DEAR HENRY,
> "You have now fairly entered the world. . . ."

An affectionate parent Lady Frances may be, but obviously the reader is not to suppose the salutation of her letter was "My dear Henry, MY DEAR HENRY." Lady Frances would not approve of such a bizarre epistolary style: the repetition is editorial.

12 Such starting-over sentences are not, in nineteenth-century literature, confined to *Kunstprosa* or the speech of the well-educated. In Jerrold's *Black-Ey'd Susan* (1828), the most successful work in that low-prestige genre, the nautical drama, we have the heroine saying, "I am poor, sir—poor and unprotected; do not, as you have children of your own, do not insult me." (I.3) Text in George Rowell's *Nineteenth Century Plays*, 2d ed. (London, 1972).

13 If we take (*a*) the fifty consecutive speeches beginning with the first in chap. 21 (the Bagstock and Mrs. Skewton chapter) and (*b*) the fifty speeches which come before Little Paul's death (i.e., from the first speech on p. 217 through Paul's last words at the end of chap. 16) and count all interruptions (that is, even such "innocent" inquits as "said he") we find that in (*a*) there are 327 words interjected by the author and in (*b*) 85 words. Since, however, our main interest in this study is in the "suspect" interjection—the interjection containing a minimum of five words—we may find it more interesting to count only these longer suspensions. In (*a*) there are 22 of these suspect interruptions, and these 22 contain 278 words. In (*b*) there are 7 suspect interruptions, and these 7 contain 55 words. (Incidentally, when a single speech is interrupted more than once—e.g., the paragraph beginning " 'What I want,' " on p. 289—I count the several interruptions individually.)

14 Here it is interesting to notice that Surtees, an *incessantly* comic novelist, exceeds even Dickens in his enthusiasm for the suspended quotation. See chap. 3 below.

15 See, e.g., *Barnaby Rudge*, chap. 74, p. 570; *Eustace Diamonds*, I, p. 40.

16 As did Sterne before them. See *Tristram Shandy*, p. 63.

17 See, e.g., *Nicholas Nickleby*, pp. 94, 116, 121, 125, 142, 177, 180, 247, 250, 271, 284, 295, 299, 307, 352. We find the device used seven times in sixty-five pages of *Dombey and Son:* pp. 566, 591, 593, 598, 625, 630 (twice).

18 On Dickens and the penny-a-liners, see below, pp. 94-95.

19 My reading of this passage is a late sprout from Steven Marcus's seminal essay, "Who is Fagin?" See Marcus's *Dickens: From Pickwick to Dombey* (New York, 1965; reprinted, 1968), pp. 358-78.

20 For example, in the first sentence of the second chapter of *Framley Parsonage*, our attention is riveted by "It will be necessary that

I should say a word or two of some of the people named in the few preceding pages, and also of the localities in which they lived." The first paragraph of the novel ended, "Mark was his eldest son and second child; and the first page or two of this narrative must be consumed in giving a catalogue of the good things which chance and conduct together had heaped upon this young man's head." The work's eighth paragraph began, "But even yet more must be told of his good fortune before we can come to the actual incidents of our story." (It is true that one page after that last sentence we are inspirited by the following: "But little has yet been said, personally, as to our hero himself, and perhaps it may not be necessary to say much. Let us hope that by degrees he may come forth upon the canvas, showing to the beholder the nature of the man inwardly and outwardly.") In another novel, *Can you Forgive Her?*, characteristically Trollopean transitions are:

> It will perhaps be as well to say a few words about Mrs. Greenlaw before we go with her to Yarmouth.
>
> [p. 76]
>
> I will give her letter at length, as I shall then be best able to proceed with my story quickly.
>
> [p. 109]
>
> But at last Alice agreed to pay this visit, and it may be as well to explain here how she was brought to do so.
>
> [p. 188]
>
> But she became aware that Mr. Palliser had been deceived. As she was right in this, we must go back for a moment, and say a word of things as they went on at Matching after Alice Vavasor had left the place.
>
> [p. 317]
>
> We may as well follow this political movement to its end.
>
> [p. 557]

21 P. 205. Characteristically, Trollope brackets this pronouncement with warnings about what happens when the novelist simply lets a conversation run on. This sort of thing will *not* be pleasing: dialogue enjoys its privileged position "only so long as it tends in some way to the telling of the main story."

22 Thanks to various forms of periodical and cheap-edition publication, a fair amount of Victorian fiction was, in fact, read, like the Bible, in two-column pages.

23 Readers of *Edwin Drood* may also wish to think about the appearance of dialogue on the page and the appearance of monumental inscriptions. The last in the Dickensian series of comic portraits of authors (the series which includes Mr. Dick) is Mr. Sapsea, and we may recall the instructions with which this character gives John Jasper his epitaph for the late Mrs. Sapsea: "Take it in your own hand. The setting out of the lines requires to be followed with the eye, as well as the content with the mind." [chap. 4, p. 36] We may well be tempted to see this vignette of authorship as cartoon self-portraiture, and we might try taking Mr. Sapsea's instructions as if they came directly from the master.

24 *The School for Scandal*, I.i.

25 On this see Louis James, *Fiction for the Working Man, 1830-50: A Study of the Literature Produced for the Working Classes in Early Victorian Urban England* (Oxford, 1963; republished London, 1974), pp. 37-39.

26 See Royal A. Gettmann, *A Victorian Publisher: A Study of the Bentley Papers* (Cambridge, England, 1960), p. 255. As Philip Gaskell points out, contracts between Victorian novelists and their publishers often specified the number of pages to be filled. (*A New Introduction to Bibliography* [Oxford, 1972], p. 301.)

27 Karl Kroeber, *Styles in Fictional Structure: The Art of Jane Austen, Charlotte Bronte, and George Eliot* (Princeton, 1971), p. 166.

28 This is not to say, of course, that a work written entirely—or almost entirely—in dialogue would be more attractive to us than a novel containing stretches of conversation within a narrative. It is the *contrast* between narration and dialogue which is essential. Dialogue is signified at the level where description is signifier, but in themselves the statements made in dialogue signify: these *are* the words Mr. Pickwick uttered in that room, but they are words *about* something.

29 Page, *Speech in the English Novel*, p. 133. In his chapter on "Dickens and Speech," Page gives us an informal but very suggestive index to the relative attractiveness of dialogue and description in Dickens. He points out that of the 262 extracts from Dickens included in the *Oxford Dictionary of Quotations*, "at least 80 percent" are from dialogue passages [p. 143]. For an example of the sort of review Page refers to, we might borrow the following *Quarterly Review* sentence (59 [1837]: 415) from George H. Ford's invaluable *Dickens & His Readers: Aspects of Novel-Criticism Since 1836* (Princeton, 1955; reprinted New York, 1965), p. 16: "The primary cause, then, of this author's success [in

*Pickwick*] we take to be his felicity in working up the genuine motherwit and unadulterated vernacular idioms of the lower classes of London."

30 See Ford's excellent discussion of Dickens and reviewers, op.cit., pp. 50–54.

31 Quoted in Preface to *The Collected Letters of Charles Dickens*, vol. 2, p. x.

32 See *Letters*, vol. 1, pp. 277, 387. For Pickwick and Nickleby examples, see vol. 1, p. 342 and p. 385. When later in life Dickens gives his public readings and uses such expressions as "I am . . . murdering Nancy," and "I do not commit the murder again . . . until Tuesday" (see Philip Collins, *Dickens and Crime* [Bloomington, 1968], pp. 267ff.), he is not doing something new but continuing something old. I am not altogether happy with Collins's suggestion that such phrases "should be understood, in the first place, as the normal mode of discourse and banter among actors" [p. 267]; Dickens started to use such expressions long before the public readings began. Here, as elsewhere, Dickens's emotions and satisfactions as a public performer are best understood as an intensification of his emotions and satisfactions as a narrator. Dickens always wants to be both in control of and in close proximity to his audience; he is *always* aggressive toward his characters.

33 Of course the entrance or disappearance of a character was not the only thing to affect monthly sales. It is well known that Dickens revived interest in *Martin Chuzzlewit* by including American episodes.

34 I do mean to imply that the character Harold Skimpole is, like many another Dickensian character, a special kind of autobiographical cartoon, a sketch of something Dickens had it in him to become. Leigh Hunt may be the model here, but he is the model because Dickens recognizes in Hunt the actualization of possibilities within himself. (Indeed, Dickens mentioned to Macrone, in a March 1836 letter [Vol. 1, p. 137], that the editor of the *Court Journal* thought Boz, the bright new author, was actually Leigh Hunt.)

It seems to me entirely right to stress, as, for instance, Taylor Stoehr does, the sense in which "Dickens seems to be *in* all his characters, to feel with and identify with them, regardless of the formal perspective finally adopted for their presentation in the novels" (*Dickens: The Dreamer's Stance* [Ithaca, 1965], pp. 44–45). But the adventure of becoming Others, becoming some of the multitudes one contains, only enhances the need for and the joy in asserting the self which lives through such adventures.

35 Forster, vol. 1, p. 52.

36 It is amusing to notice that Dickens played with the speaker's power over the scribe when he taught his own son shorthand. Henry Dickens would be made to take down speeches declaimed by his father, but, as Sir Henry was to recall, the elder Dickens "would insist . . . on adding to my difficulties by the character of the speeches he delivered—speeches of an absurdly ridiculous and bombastic kind, mock travesties of those which in years gone by he had been in the habit of listening to in the Gallery of the House of Commons. Dear me, how well I remember how he made me laugh! But that was not the worst of it, because whilst I was struggling with my laughter his denunciation of his imaginary opponent increased in volume and intensity. So much so, indeed, that between the two I was soon reduced to a state of helpless imbecility." Sir Henry Dickens, K.C., *Memories of My Father* (London, 1928), p. 27.

37 My knowledge of the monopolylogue comes almost exclusively from Philip Collins's *Reading Aloud: A Victorian Métier* (Lincoln, England, 1972) and the third chapter of Davis's *The Flint and the Flame*.

38 *Reading Aloud*, pp. 25–26.

39 Johnson, vol. 1, p. 735. For the text of *Mr. Nightingale's Diary*, see the second volume of *The Plays and Poems of Charles Dickens*, edited by Richard Herne Shepherd, 2 vols. (London, 1885).

40 *Victorian Novelists and Publishers* (Chicago, 1976), p. 166.

41 "Dickens is the artist as tycoon, dedicated to building up an impregnable personal empire, literary, domestic, financial." Introduction to *The Selected Letters of Charles Dickens* (New York, 1960), p. xi. Our modern, very strong awareness of what Dupee elsewhere in this passage calls "Dickens' tremendous will to power" probably begins with the observations of Humphry House in *The Dickens World* (first published in London, 1941): "There was a strong authoritarian strain in [Dickens]. . . ." "He had an almost fanatical devotion to the Metropolitan Police." "There are many reasons for believing that he belonged to the Freudian 'anal type,' obsessed with neatness and precision." (2d ed., Oxford, 1960, pp. 201–03). What I am arguing here, of course, is that Dickens's authoritarianism and will to power are not simply facts of the author's life, or ideas useful for an understanding of some social

attitudes to be inferred from the novels: they are parts *of* the novels, things to which we respond when we read. We must understand our readerly (as distinct from our social) response to these things in the novel if we are to think further about "the Dickens experience."

42 G. W. Turner, *Stylistics* (Baltimore, 1973), p. 123.

43 On this see Stephen C. Gill, " 'Pickwick Papers' and the 'Chroniclers by the Line': a Note on Style," *MLR* 63 (1968): 33–36. The hack novelists's trick of writing a good deal of dialogue is of course more efficient than the penny-a-liner's inflated diction, in that the novelist can claim a line without having to fill it up. In any case, there is no reason to think Dickens actually used either of these Grub Street tricks simply to fill up a sheet: in point of fact, he was more likely to overwrite than underwrite the available space. What interests us is the shabby-genteel associations of that ornate style which so fascinated Dickens. The style is richly equivocal: it separates one from anything low, is urbane, but on the other hand suggests both a Micawberesque wish to draw back from reality and a Grub Street desire to gain a few extra pennies with which to deal with reality.

I stress Dickens's probable double-vision of his own ornate style the more because it would appear that outsiders—the great world—judged his narrational style in two quite different ways. The early theme—even among those who praised Dickensian lower-class dialogue—that the Dickensian narrative voice is vulgar, its language imperfect, crude, journalistic, starts with the reviews of *Pickwick* and continues through Dickens's lifetime—especially when Dickens is compared with Thackeray. (See Ford, pp. 113–15.) Opinions of this kind are important not only for our understanding of Dickens's reputation but for our understanding of Dickens's sense of himself: the prefaces Dickens wrote for his novels are, as Ford points out [p. 52], pretty strong witnesses to Dickens's awareness of adverse criticism. On the other hand, there were always those who recognized the fact that Dickens was a great master of English prose. Dr. Henry Danson, who had been a contemporary at the Wellington Academy, is obviously not thinking about the speeches of Sam Weller or Sarah Gamp when he writes, "Depend on it [Dickens] was quite a self-made man, and his wonderful knowledge and command of the English language must have been acquired by long and patient study after leaving his last school." [Forster, vol. 1, p. 41] One should also mention here Dickens's reputation as a superb after-dinner speaker. It seems a reasonable guess that Dickens was highly aware of both views of his personal style, and that the double-evaluation encouraged him to be at once easy and competitive in his prose.

Finally I should direct the reader's attention to the discussion of ornate and inflated diction in Garrett Stewart's *Dickens and the Trials of Imagination* (Cambridge, Mass., 1974) and to the paragraphs on the Dickensian "genteel-facetious" voice in A. O. J. Cockshut's *The Imagination of Charles Dickens* (New York, 1962), p. 86. No one makes a better case than Stewart for the deeply satiric intent of at least much of Dickens's fancy talk; Cockshut seems to me right in suggesting that Dickens's liking for that genteel-facetious tone has complex psychological causes.

44 No reader is likely to misattribute any of the speeches here to Molly—even momentarily. It would, however, be somewhat tedious to show precisely why this is so.

45 See chap. 3 below.

46 Sylvère Monod is struck by the frequency of tags in *David Copperfield:* in a stretch of thirteen chapters of that novel, Monod finds only nineteen speeches without some kind of identifying tag. *Dickens the Novelist*, with an Introduction by Edward Wagenknecht (Norman, Okla., 1968), p. 342. Monod also points to something quite interesting which we shall be turning to in a few moments: Dickens's tendency to add a second identification of the speaker, a second tag, at or near the end of a longish speech.

47 Cf. Roman Jakobson: "There are messages primarily serving to establish, to prolong, or to discontinue communication, to check whether the channel works ('Hello, do you hear me?'), to attract the attention of the interlocutor or to confirm his continued attention. . . . This set for CONTACT, or in Malinowski's terms PHATIC function . . . may be displayed by a profuse exchange of ritualized formulas, by entire dialogues with the mere purport of prolonging communication. . . . The endeavor to start and sustain communication is typical of talking birds; thus the phatic function of language is the only one they share with human beings. It is also the first verbal function acquired by infants; they are prone to communicate before they are able to send or receive information communication." "Linguistics and Poetics," in *Style in Language*, ed. Thomas A. Sebeok (Cambridge, Mass., 1960); reprinted in *The Structuralists: From Marx to Levi-Strauss*, ed. Richard and Fernande DeGeorge (Garden City, N. Y., 1972), p. 92. See also

Turner's *Stylistics*, pp. 209-13. Phatic language, it should be noted, can have an informational content, as in the case of a passage Jakobson quotes from a Dorothy Parker story ("Well, here we are") or "lovely weather we're having" or, as I am suggesting, "said he" or "she replied." These messages need not be regarded as mere "pseudo-messages" or "prop messages." John Lyons is sensibly cautious about disregarding the information-conveying function of utterances which also have a function in "phatic communion": "we recognize that, even when both of these are present, either one or the other may be the dominant part of the 'use' of the utterance." *Introduction to Theoretical Linguistics* (Cambridge, England, 1969), p. 417. It is this doubleness of function in Dickensian speech-tags which makes their frequent repetition affecting, but not cloying, smothering.

48 In this respect the exchange I have quoted here seems fairly typical of *Nicholas Nickleby*. In a group of three runs of 100 tagged speeches in that novel (beginning with the openings of chap. 3, chap. 38, and chap. 59) *said* is used about half the time: 145 occurrences. Next comes *replied* (64 occurrences), *returned* (18), and only then does a suprasegmental verb, *cried*, appear (14 occurrences). *Asked* is used 9 times, and *inquired*, with 8 occurrences, is the sixth most frequently used tag-verb. We do have 6 uses of *muttered*, 2 each of *bawled*, *growled*, and *exclaimed*, and the odd *sighed* and *hiccuped*. On the whole, though, our small but I believe representative sampling suggests a less "lyric" set of speech-verbs than we would find in a number of eighteenth-century novels. (See chap. 1, n. 8.) As I have suggested before, *cry* tends to be the most important resource of and evidence for "lyrical" tagging in the eighteenth and early nineteenth centuries.

49 See n. 46.

50 Cf. Page, p. 29: "[There is a] convention, much favoured by Jane Austen, whereby the novelist is permitted to conflate into a single speech what must probably be supposed to have been uttered as several separate speeches."

51 For other examples of the booster-shot identification in the two novels we've been citing, see, in *Nicholas Nickleby*, pp. 61, 74, 94, 115, 199, 227, 250-51, 273, 340, 446, and in *Dombey and Son*, pp. 419, 535, 539, 546, 556, 565, 567, 579, 581, 589, 596, 598, 607, 615, 616, 616-17, 622, 629.

52 For some other examples of the late explanation, see *PP*, 411; *NN*, 387, 538, 735; *BR*, 219, 574; *MC*, 138-39; *DS*, 329, 426-27.

53 *The Maturity of Dickens* (Cambridge, Mass., 1959), p. 4.

54 *The Narrative Art of Charles Dickens* (Oxford, 1970), chap. 1.

55 When considering authorial resentment in Dickens, one might ponder an interesting remark Philip Collins makes about Dickens as a public reader: "On the few occasions when a performance fell short of success, [Dickens] generally blames the dullness of the audience. Never does he make the self-analysis or express the self-criticism that one finds in, say, the diaries of W. C. Macready." ("Dickens' Self-Estimate: Some New Evidence," in *Dickens the Craftsman: Strategies of Presentation*, ed. Robert B. Partlow, Jr. [Carbondale and Edwardsville, Ill., 1970], p. 23.) If one takes the face-to-face public performances as less a new or different thing for Dickens than a simplification and intensification of his authorial experience, Collins's remark is highly suggestive—the more so if one recalls the first paragraph of Dickens's Preface to the Cheap Edition of *Martin Chuzzlewit:*

> What is exaggeration to one class of minds and perceptions is plain truth to another. That which is commonly called a long-sight, perceives in a prospect innumerable features and bearings non-existent to a short-sighted person. I sometimes ask myself whether there may occasionally be a difference of this kind between some writers and some readers: whether it is *always* the writer who colours highly, or whether it is now and then the reader whose eye for colour is a little dull?

56 By way of contrast, one can hardly find anything more instructive than such a passage as this from that Dickensian favorite, *Tom Jones:*

> And now, Reader, as we are in haste to attend our Heroine, we will leave to thy Sagacity to apply all this to the *Boeotian* Writers, and to those Authors who are their Opposites. This thou wilt be abundantly able to perform without our Aid. Bestir thyself therefore on this Occasion; for tho' we will always lend thee proper Assistance in difficult Places, as we do not, like some others, expect thee to use the Art of Divination to discover our Meaning; yet we shall not indulge thy Laziness where nothing but thy own Attention is required; for thou art highly mistaken if thou dost imagine that we intended, when we began this great Work, to leave thy Sagacity nothing to do; or that, without sometimes exercising this Talent, thou wilt be able to travel through our Pages with any Pleasure or Profit to thyself.
>
> [IX, 9, p. 469]

This passage and others like it are quoted in the admirable chapter on Fielding in Wolfgang Iser's *The Implied Reader: Patterns of Communication in Prose Fiction from Bunyan to Beckett* (Baltimore, 1974). Though that discussion of Fielding does not even touch on Dickens, it has much to teach anyone who comes to it soon after a reading of Dickens. Fielding, one of the masters, does insist that the reader *work.* One need not agree with everything Iser says to realize that such a paragraph as the one just quoted, even if it is thought to be only half in earnest, sets up a relationship between novelist and reader that would simply be impossible, unthinkable in Dickens.

## CHAPTER THREE

1 Originally published in *The Nation* 1 (1865): 786–87. Reprinted in *The Dickens Critics*, ed. George H. Ford and Lauriat Lane, Jr. (Ithaca, 1961), pp. 48–54.
2 *Charles Dickens: His Life and Work* (New York, 1936), p. 137.
3 In his discussion of *Great Expectations* Barry Westburg also draws attention to that knowledge of Dickens's earlier novels with which a reader would come to the newest one. See *The Confessional Fictions of Charles Dickens* (Dekalb, Ill., 1977), p. 187.
4 *Language of Fiction: Essays in Criticism and Verbal Analysis of the English Novel* (New York, 1967), p. 151.
5 Compare Karl Kroeber's remarks on George Eliot's mixed dialogue-and-narrative sentences and the relation of these to the slow reading her novels demand. *Styles in Fictional Structure*, p. 176.
6 Quoted by Dingle Foot in his Introduction to the Oxford Illustrated Dickens *Hard Times*, p. vii.
7 For a discussion along rather different lines of the influence of Dickens's public readings upon his late style, see Page's *Speech in the English Novel*, pp. 135–37.

It should be remembered, by the way, that though the public readings—the solo performances of and by Charles Dickens—do not begin until 1853, more conventional, less purely egocentric theatricals had long interested him, and amateur performances may already have been of some importance in his emotional life. Cf. Edgar Johnson's biography, p. 644: "Gradually Dickens had come to feel himself haunted by a specter of his own unhappiness. Throughout the five months following the completion of *Dombey* he managed to keep up his spirits by the violent stimulations of stage directing and acting. Then, as soon as they were over, he subsided again into outcries of misery."

## APPENDIX 1

1 For a brief discussion of this and other forms of lack of concord in Dickensian dialogue, see G. L. Brook, *The Language of Dickens* (London, 1970), pp. 242–43.
2 I paraphrase here Saul Levin's "The Vulgar Historical Present in *-s*," *JEGP* 48 (1949): 127–31.
3 Quoted from John Ashton's *Humour, Wit and Satire of the Seventeenth Century* (London, 1883; republished New York, 1968), p. 407.
4 Quoted from *Journals of Dorothy Wordsworth*, edited and with an Introduction by Helen Darbishire (London, 1958).
5 II, 345–50. Quoted from Francis Beaumont's *The Knight of the Burning Pestle*, ed. John Doebler (Lincoln, Nebr., 1967).
6 Ed. Chester G. Anderson, (New York, 1964), pp. 36–37.
7 Ed. James Sutherland (Boston, 1959), p. 25.
8 New York, 1948, chap. 2, p. 7.
9 Chap. 32, p. 208.

In a paragraph from Hunter S. Thompson's *Fear and Loathing in Las Vegas* (originally published 1971) we find the complementary situation: the narrative *-s* introduced to tag a direct quotation but used for the next finite verb as well. (Here matters are slightly but unimportantly complicated by the authorial "He laughed," which comes between the two *-s* forms):

> "Hah! That's a *bitch*, ain't it?" the H-D boomer shouted to nobody in particular. "Last night I was out home in Long Beach and somebody said they were runnin' the Mint 400 today, so I says to my old lady, 'Man, I'm goin'." He laughed. "So she gives me a lot of crap about it, you know . . . so I started slappin' her around and the next thing I knew two guys I never even seen before got me out on the sidewalk workin' me over. Jesus! They beat me stupid."
>
> [New York, n.d. chap. 5, p. 35]

Note the suspension in this paragraph.

10 Sutherland, p. 23.
11 On this use of the dramatic present in popular narration, see Otto Jespersen, *The Philosophy of Grammar* (1924; New York, 1965), p. 258.

12 For a rather different appraoch to this topic, but one which does seem, like mine, to emphasize a sort of privileged status directly quoted words are given in colloquial narration, see Christian Paul Casparis, *Tense without Time: The Present Tense in Narration* (Bern, 1975), pp. 116–19.

In the recently published "The Conversational Historical Present Alternation" (*Language* 55 [1979]: 168–82) Nessa Wolfson maintains that in the collection of conversational modern English narratives she has examined (that is, in a group of accurately recorded *spoken* narratives, rather than novelistic imitations of such narratives) there is no correlation between use of the present tense and any special vividness or importance of content. According to Wolfson, what is significant is not the use of past tense or present tense per se but a switch from whichever of the two is being employed to the other when the speaker wishes to mark off one part of a story from another. Particularly interesting for us is the author's observation that speakers tend not to switch tenses in a set of coordinate sentences: in such sets, verbs of motion and of speaking will be in the same tense. (Wolfson does point out that the verb *say* is used in ways which create special problems of explanation; but the difficulties Wolfson mentions are not quite the ones we might have expected.) "The Conversational Historical Present Alternation" is a stimulating paper, and I am by no means sure (though I may suspect) that Wolfson is wrong about how and why most speakers of modern English use the historical present. But of course Wolfson's concerns are not quite ours. What matters most for us is not the facts of tense switching in late twentieth-century conversations but what writers of the past few centuries seem to have thought the facts of English conversation to be. Whatever it may do for contemporary American talk, Wolfson's analysis neither is nor claims to be the most useful guide to tense switching in, for example, *Huckleberry Finn*.

## APPENDIX 2

1 See Fish's article, cited in chap. 1, n. 1.

2 If one were interested, for instance, in what A. Q. Morton calls "stylometry"—the measurement of style for purposes of testing claims to authorship—one would do much more with statistical data like those collected here; indeed, stylometry *is* a use of measurements of the style of a text. See Morton's *Literary Detection: How to Prove Authorship and Fraud in Literature and Documents* (New York, 1978).

# Index